PEEL

GAME

*A Woman's Guide to Unmasking
Mr. Wrong and Finding Mr. Right!*

David Brackins

ISBN: 979-8-89298-662-5 [Paper Back]

ISBN: 979-8-89298-664-9 [eBook]

Published by Cox Press Publishing Media.

1317 Edgewater Dr #2614

Orlando FL 3280

Follow me on social media:
Facebook: https://www.facebook.com/DavidBrackins0624
Instagram: https://www.instagram.com/davidbrackins0624
TikTok: https://www.tiktok.com/@davidbrackins0624

Table of Contents

Dedication

This book is lovingly dedicated to two pillars of strength and inspiration in my life: To my dear wife, whose patience and grace were the calm in my creative storms. Your unwavering faith in my vision gave me the peace and motivation my soul needed to write these pages. Every word is a testament to the enduring love and generous spirit that you embody. To my precious daughter, who, from the moment you graced this world with your presence, inspired a profound transformation in me. Your birth was the spark that ignited my desire to be the best man I could be, not just for you and your future but as a beacon for other men striving for change. And to all the courageous women who have tasted the bitter pain of heartbreak, may the bruises on your hearts guide you towards a love that not only heals but also exalts your spirit. This book aspires to be a companion on your journey toward healing and a testament to the resolute power of love and self-discovery. May this narrative honor your experiences, resonate with your struggles, empower your choices, and celebrate the relentless hope that dwells within every woman's heart. Together, may we march towards a future where love's power triumphs over its trials.

Introduction

Mr. Red Flag

Navigating genuine and authentic connections in to-day's world can be quite challenging. We find ourselves in a society where the rules of love have undergone a complete rewrite. The value placed on relationships and societal norms has significantly diminished. With the arrival of dating apps that offer swiping left or right, finding a date has become comparable to shopping. Don't get me wrong, having choices can be empowering, but it's easy to fall into the trap of feeling disposable. I don't mean to sound pessimistic, but I am aware that the dating pool is shallow and murky, filled with immature men who most likely lacked proper male role models growing up. Many lack integrity and have formed dating concepts from movies or music artists they admire. The game has evolved, and viable options seem to be few and far between. In this modern dating era, behaviors like ghosting, drama with baby mamas, and engaging in multiple relationships simultaneously have become the new norm. Unfortunately, only a small number of men truly comprehend and desire to pursue long-term relationships with marriage in mind. But most men find themselves hopping from one relationship to another, perpetually believing that the grass is always greener on the other side. Today's men often approach dating as a type of romantic musical chair, where multiple women are in constant rotation, fitting into their distorted perception of love. However, many hearts are left broken, bruised, and disillusioned when the music stops. I must admit, I have only experienced one side of heartbreak—the side that breaks hearts. I was, to put it bluntly, a walking red flag during my single days. It brings me no pride to confess that in the past, whether in somewhat long-term relationships or situationships, I had a talent for misleading or, at times, outright lying to women in order to fulfill my own desires. But I want to clarify that this is not a badge of honor. Rather, it is an acknowledgment of my own personal failings. Although I am only 38, I have unfortunately witnessed and engaged in various game-playing and commitment evasion forms. I have experienced it all, and now I feel compelled to share what I have learned from being on the other side of the dating spectrum.

From Wild Nights to a Wise Love

When I look back at my journey and the person I used to be, I can't help but cringe a little. I was quite the character—a self-centered, "love 'em and leave 'em" kind of guy who treated love as a game, moving from one relationship to another without any real commitment. It was all about pleasure and putting myself first. Vulnerability was a trap I avoided, keeping my emotions at a distance. Looking back now, I see how flawed my perspective on dating and relationships was, but I was blind to the consequences of my actions. Deep down, I knew I couldn't continue living as a womanizer forever. But I didn't honestly believe I was capable of change. That's when I did what I've always done when I felt lost, afraid, or confused. I turned to God, seeking guidance from a higher power. The wisdom I found in God's principles opened my eyes to the darkness I had been carrying and illuminated the truth. I realized that my promiscuous lifestyle was a cover-up for deeper issues I had been avoiding. I felt a newfound sense of responsibility and commitment on my journey of self-discovery. I confronted my demons and reflected on the suppressed experiences from my past. I recognized the impact of the dysfunctional relationships I had considered normal and the deep wounds they had caused. It wasn't an instant transformation, but eventually, I forgave myself. That forgiveness was the key to unlocking compassion and empathy within me that I never knew existed. I was determined to break free from my destructive and selfish patterns that were hindering my personal growth and preventing meaningful relationships. Today, I am a completely transformed man. I am grateful, humbled, and, most importantly, I have learned from my mistakes. I now understand genuine love is not a fairy tale or a game. It is a powerful force that can heal and enrich lives. I realized that commitment and emotional involvement are not signs of weakness but foundations for personal growth and expressing real, authentic love. My past was filled with red flags, warning signs I had ignored. It took some courage to confront my own emotional wounds and face them head-on. The selfishness and serial dating are behind me now. My messy past has shaped me into someone who appreciates the opportunity to grow and become a better person. My focus is on being there for others and positively impacting their lives. During this journey of self-discovery, I found my soulmate.

She is an incredible woman who saw beyond my flaws and embraced the transformation within me. She did not judge me for my past but saw that I could improve. Her love and support inspired me to use my experiences for good and to share my unique perspective. With her by my side, I faced my flaws, took ownership of my past, and embraced the person I was evolving into. So here I am, my reckless days behind me, grateful for the lessons learned and the wise love that guided me to this responsible present. It wasn't an easy road, but it was worth every step. I am fully committed if my past and the cautionary tales I share can help others avoid those red flags and find genuine connections. Life offers no guarantees, but with faith, insight, and self-awareness, it is possible to turn things around and discover the love one truly deserves.

A Friend's Request

Picture this: I was lying in bed with my wife, just casually browsing social media, when, out of the blue, she dropped a request on me. It seemed innocent enough at the time. She mentioned that one of her friends, whom I was acquainted with, was seeking dating advice from a male perspective. I thought to myself, "Sure, why not? I have some insights to share." Little did I know that this seemingly simple favor would take me on an unexpected journey. A few days later, I found myself having a heart-to-heart with my wife's friend as she poured out her relationship issues. I attentively listened, nodding along while doing my best to analyze the information she shared about her situation. I responded honestly, sharing my thoughts from a male's perspective as if I were speaking to my sister or a close female cousin. She genuinely appreciated my candid insights. Word quickly spread, and before I knew it, I was conversing with not just one but three of my wife's friends, each facing unique relationship struggles. These women were intelligent and came from different backgrounds. Yet, I was surprised to discover they were all grappling with the same problem—their partners displayed severe red flags. These were the kind of warning signs that screamed, "Danger ahead! Stop!" While offering advice, I couldn't help but reflect on my questionable past. I've had my fair share of moments I'm not proud of, but then it hit me: sharing my own stories could become a lifeline for these ladies and countless others. I realized that this knowledge shouldn't be confined to private conversations between friends; it should be shared with the public. I wanted to help other women avoid relationship disasters by identifying men who play games and waste their time. With a sincere desire to make a difference, I delved deep into my experiences, even the cringeworthy ones, to provide valuable insights. It was as if I had turned my past mistakes into a superpower, guiding these women through the complexities of dating and exposing game-playing behaviors. And that's how this book came to be. I poured my energy into creating a comprehensive guide outlining seven warning signs in men that should not be ignored. So, if you're wondering how I went from a guy with a checkered history to offering my perspective on dating, it all began with a simple request. Life has a funny way of surprising us, doesn't it? You never know when inspiration will strike and turn everything around. Now, I'm on a mission to help women learn from my mistakes and avoid falling into the same old traps.

Purpose of the book

I'm sure, like most women, you have been played on some level once or twice, maybe even a third time. Even celebrities with all their beauty and wealth get played just the same; if it can happen to them, anyone can get it. Now, you might wonder, "Who the heck does this handsome, dapper man think he is to tell me how to navigate my love life?" Let me start by saying that I am not a relationship guru with a halo over my head, nor do I pretend to have all the answers on dating. But I've been in the trenches and seen these overlooked red flags firsthand in relationships and in the scenarios shared by my wife's friends. Trust me, these patterns aren't just isolated incidents. There are plenty of Mr. Wrongs lurking out there, waiting to trip you up. To be clear, this isn't your typical run-of-the-mill relationship advice book. This isn't for the city girls having a hot girl summer, and I'm not here to feed you clichés or give you tired, old, recycled lines. Oh no, this book is for women looking for Mr. Right and tired of dating blindly, falling for the same old tricks, and getting the same results. Unlike most books about dating, I refuse to give you a generic, watered-down, and gimmicky rendition. Instead, I plan on diving deep into the murky waters of dating and relationships and, most importantly, exposing the sneaky mind games men play that you should never ignore! So, what's this book all about? Empowering women with the knowledge and insight that only a reformed playboy could provide to help spot those deceitful wolves in sheep's clothing. We're not just talking about the usual suspects; we're talking about Mr. Hobosexual, who's just in it for the money ride, and Mr. Potential, the master of empty promises. But I'm not stopping there! I've got more game to reveal. How about Mr. Aimless, the dude with no sense of direction or ambition? Or is Mr. Dream Seller the one peddling fantasy instead of reality? And, oh, let's not overlook Mr. Secretive, the mysterious man hiding all his skeletons in the closet. Fear not, ladies; I won't leave you hanging. Each of these individuals has what I like to call red flag tendencies. We'll dive deep into their twisted characteristics and motivations. We'll even explore the wreckage they can cause in your once-promising relationships. But we won't just point out the problems; we will arm you with practical solutions. That's right! Step-by-step instructions to help you spot these men from a mile away and steer clear of their toxic paths. But wait! Let me clarify before you think we're here to hate on all men. This isn't about bashing men or giving up on love altogether, nor is it about feeding the myth that there's no good man left in the world. Oh no, it's about taking charge and making informed decisions aligning with your values and dreams. You're the queen who deserves a king who provides you with nothing but the absolute best. So, let's take this journey together—unmasking those wolves, shielding your heart, and guiding you toward genuine, nurturing, and everlasting love. This ain't no fairytale, but with this book in your hands, you'll be armed with wisdom and ready to conquer the dating game.

Chapter 1:

♟

Mr. Dream Seller: Don't Buy It!

"Beware of those who sell dreams, for their promises are often empty and their intentions unclear."
— David Brackins

I n the complicated world of dating, there exists a peculiar group of men that I call dream sellers. These are very confident and charming guys who are so persuasive they can trick women, no matter how smart or experienced they are. These men come in two different types. The first is Type A (long-term); he makes compelling plans for the future to capture your heart. The second is Type B (short-term), who loves short, passionate flings full of excitement. No matter what type they are, these men are good at playing mind games that can confuse you and make you fall for their promises, creating a lot of emotional mess. But don't worry; I'm here to help. I will teach you to spot these tricky men from far away before they can draw you into their lies. My advice will help you understand how to avoid these guys' tricks and teach you how to protect your feelings as you figure out the complicated world of love and relationships.

Exposing the Type A Dream Seller

Let's start with Type A dream seller. This dude is slick. He's really good at mixing a bit of truth with lots of big promises about a future that always seems just around the corner. He'll tell you stories of what he plans to do, mixing in enough real action to make you believe that these amazing things he discusses are within your reach. He will also use your hopes of a healthy relationship to make it seem like you're both working toward the same goal. But as you get sucked into his only half-true stories, it gets hard to distinguish the truth from the fear that starts creeping in. And that's how you learn that not every dream sold to you is meant to be pursued. Instead of using beautiful words to entangle you in a web of deception, real men who want a relationship have goals, milestones, and a path to success. So, when you encounter a Type A dream seller, pay attention to the gap between what he promised and the plan presented to reach it. If one's missing, you might just be buying into a dream built to never be caught—a future always out of reach, vibrant but vanishing as you stretch your hands to grasp it. Usually, if he's been with you long enough, he will know which buttons to push to play on your emotions and fears and keep you wrapped around his finger.

Recognizing The Signs: Type A's Playbook

Picture this: You're already deep into a long-term relationship with a Type A dream seller who is a master of excuses, always having a ready-made story for his inconsistencies. When you confront him about his behavior or lack of effort, he weaves a web of words to keep you trapped. But he's just running away from resolving issues and discussing the future. Let's explore the behaviors of the Type A dream seller.

Master of Excuses: When you call him out, he's got a ready-made excuse for every occasion. His creativity knows no bounds regarding justifying why he can't show up or be there for you. *Example:* "Babe, I know I've been distant lately, but I'm dealing with some personal issues. I need space to sort things out before fully focusing on our relationship."

Comfort in Complacency: As the relationship drifts towards oblivion, he's unfazed. He'd rather coast in an unsatisfying situation than make an effort to change or improve things. *Example:* You talk to him about your feelings, and he shrugs it off, saying, "Bae, we're comfortable together, and that's what matters most. Why rock the boat by trying to change things?"

Master of Emotional Manipulation: When you threaten to leave, he plays on your fear of being alone to keep you around. He knows just how to tug at your heartstrings to make you stay. *Example:* He'll say things like, "I can't imagine my life without you, and I'll do whatever it takes to make it work. Nobody else cares about me like you do. I'm a mess without you, baby."

The Slouch: He's a champion at delaying conversations about the future or resolving issues. Instead of facing these issues head-on, he procrastinates, hoping that they will somehow vanish without any effort on his part. ***Example:*** You've been asking him to discuss moving in together, and he keeps saying, I promise I'll think about it, but can we please not have this conversation right now? "Let's talk about it later, babe."

Pause for a moment and ask yourself:

1. Does your man always have an excuse ready when you call him out on his inconsistency?
2. Does he brush off serious conversations about the future like it's no big deal?
3. And when you threaten to leave, does he hit you with those guilt-tripping lines?

If you answered "yes" to any of these, you might be dealing with a Type A dream seller. It may be time to have an honest conversation with yourself as well as your partner and decide whether this relationship is truly fulfilling your needs and happiness?

Kerri and the Illusion of love

Let me share a real-life story to bring this lesson to life. Consider the case of Kerri, who fell for Tim, a stereotypical Type A dream seller. Tim promised marriage, a bright future, and a fairy tale romance at the beginning of their involvement. Because Kerri was deeply drawn to the vision he spun, she embraced his promises without demanding consistent action or a track record of keeping his word. Given her emotional vulnerability and desire for commitment, Tim exploited these attributes by painting an idea of a picture-perfect relationship. Dream sellers like Tim prey on the trust of women who take their words at face value, and unfortunately, due to Kerri's gullibility, she did exactly that. Once committed to the dream, she found herself investing increasingly in the relationship. At the same time, Tim gave nothing in return—offering no ring, no security, and yet benefiting as Kerri played the role of a devoted partner. Tim never took any real initiative, did the bare minimum, and failed to nurture the bond or deliver on his lavish promises. Kerri, overlooking all the warning signs and manipulative tactics Tim used to gain her trust, didn't recognize that she was entrenched in a doomed relationship. Over time, despite more investment from her side, substantial problems in the relationship went unaddressed. Ultimately, Kerri faced the harsh truth that she'd been taken advantage of, a realization that came with deep regret. Looking back, she could have avoided this painful outcome by allowing herself time to heal from past wounds, questioning promises critically, and displaying healthy skepticism towards extravagant claims lacking proof. Moreover, being alert to issues like commitment phobia or Tim's lack of investment could have been significant. Take note from Kerri's story, ladies, and remember: There's never any harm in leaving a situation that's not aligned with your best interests.

Exposing the Type B Dream Seller

Right from the start, this smooth talker differs significantly from his Type A counterpart. He is only in it for a quick thrill and an even quicker exit. When he's interested in someone romantically, he attempts to use your desires, needs, or fantasies to sleep with you (the first night, if possible). He wants to know what you deeply wish for or dream about, and he'll use what he finds out to make you feel special, hoping you'll be interested in him right away. He's very good at making you feel like the most special person on earth. By asking deep questions and listening carefully, he seems like he's really interested in you. But it's all just a trick. He acts like the perfect match for you while quietly trying to get physically close to you. His smooth ways hide the fact that he only wants a quick relationship, and he gives many empty compliments and promises just to get what he wants. Eventually, you may notice that his interest isn't as strong, and he doesn't contact you much anymore. It's usually around this time that you figure out that this show of romance is all fake. All that's left once he's gone is the memory of his temporary signs of affection.

Recognizing The Signs: Type B's Playbook

Charm-drenched Conversationalist: A smooth talker who can sweep you off your feet with charming words. He can make even the simplest conversation feel like a dance, leaving you mesmerized and enchanted. *Example:* He effortlessly compliments you, making you feel like the most desirable person in the room, but be cautious of excessive flattery without genuine substance.

Elusive Commitment: He avoids commitment like a plague, keeping your status vague and uncertain. ***Example:*** He will dodge conversations about the future while deflecting any talk regarding establishing exclusivity, leaving you hanging.

Fantasy Playground Creator: While in the early stages of dating, they'll listen to your desires and turn them into manipulation tools, leading you down a path you never intended to follow. ***Example:*** He might listen intently to your dreams of traveling and experiencing adventures and then pretend to share the same desires or provide access to that lifestyle to manipulate you into sleeping with him.

Pause for a moment and ask yourself:

1. How often do you rush into relationships, overlooking potential red flags?

2. Can you distinguish between heartfelt compliments and a shiny facade hiding empty intentions?

3. Have you ever been lured into a relationship that seemed too good to be true?

4. How can you protect yourselves from being drawn into a manipulator's fantasy world?

5. Have you ever hesitated to enforce your boundaries because you were afraid of scaring someone away? How did that turn out?

Here's an example of a Type B guy in action:

Nicole and the Mirage of Excitement

Let's meet Nicole and Gary, the perfect example of a dangerous dance between a Type B dream seller and an unsuspecting victim. They crossed paths several times at a bar before exchanging their contact information. They were both attracted to each other and dated for about a month. Nicole, a homebody at heart, laid her life bare before Gary, sharing her desires and vulnerabilities during their conversations. She explained how her life can sometimes be boring due to her focus on her career, and she would like to be more adventurous. She goes into detail while Gary asks more intimate questions and listens intently. Little did she know Gary was a master manipulator, gathering this information as ammunition that he would later use to convince Nicole that he could provide what she desired most. The sad reality is that she fell into Gary's trap. In a short time, he had her sold on a dream she didn't even know she was buying. With a few dates, he created a mirage of excitement tailored to a fake adventurous lifestyle that he knew would ignite her curiosity and emotions. Soon, things between the two heated up quickly, and she granted him access to her body multiple times without questioning if he was genuine. However, as fast as the flame between them ignited, he abruptly ghosted her for someone else he met after their last session. Nicole tried reaching out to Gary several times, only to find that he had blocked her phone number and access to all his social media. Left used, embarrassed, and without closure, all Nicole could do was endure the betrayal that could've possibly been avoided with careful observation and a little patience. The Type B dream seller might be enchanting, but a potential world of hurt lies beneath the surface. From the very beginning, Gary's goal was to sleep with Nicole ASAP. He accomplished this after a few conversations and took her out on a couple of mediocre dates outside of her comfort zone. Nicole learned the hard way that actions speak louder than words. As you arm yourself with knowledge and self-awareness, you can better protect your heart and make wiser choices.

Peep Game: Testing for Pure Gold

Did you know that one of the ways for a jeweler to determine pure gold from fake bling is to conduct an acid test? The jeweler would repeatedly place tiny drops of strong acid on the metal's surface to test its authenticity. The importance of this test shouldn't be overlooked, as it is used to identify pure gold from mere junk. You can apply a similar approach to dating. Imagine metaphorically that each drop of acid represents your standards and boundaries. That gold, well, that's your potential partner's true intentions. Every time the acid hits that gold, you can observe their actions, consistency, dedication, and how invested they are in making the relationship work. Take some time and be clear about your own values and expectations. You cannot apply the 'acid test' without knowing what you're testing for. This requires honest self-reflection and a strong sense of self-awareness. Next, communicate your standards early on. There's no point in waiting to see if someone will guess them correctly. Setting these standards helps you quickly identify compatible individuals in the grand scheme of things. Remember, the right partner will respect your boundaries and even share similar ideals. Keeping the gold metaphor in mind, strive for someone who doesn't corrode under the acid of your expectations but shines even brighter. So, let's dive in with some actionable tips you can apply!

1. **Take It Easy:** No need to rush into anything physical or emotional, sis. Let that relationship simmer and develop naturally to give yourself time to assess your feelings and see if it's the real deal. **Think about it:** Don't let the heat of the moment cloud your judgment. Get to know each other deeper before you dive headfirst into intimacy.

2. **Know Your Worth and Value:** Recognize your self-worth. You're a queen, and you should be treated like one. Set your standards high and demand the respect, consideration, and care you deserve. Understand that you are worthy of respect in any relationship. **Ask Yourself**: What are my core values? What are my deal-breakers? Keep that list close, and check it when unsure about a potential partner. Take time for self-reflection and identify your core values.

3. **Set Boundaries and Enforce Them:** You must lay down the ground rules! Make it clear from the jump what's acceptable regarding physical contact, communication, and emotional expectations. And hey, if those lines get crossed, stand your ground and enforce those boundaries. **Remember This:** Communication is the

name of the game. Don't be afraid to speak up and assert yourself when someone oversteps your boundaries.

Having non-negotiable standards and firm boundaries means holding yourself accountable, and it's a surefire way to protect your heart and time from those dream sellers. The acid test is a reminder to be patient and skeptical when someone promises the world but delivers little. Watch their moves! Remember, true gold stands the test of time, and a real partner will prove their worth with consistent actions and unwavering dedication. So, peep game, sis, and conduct your own acid test to ensure you find someone genuinely golden.

Chapter 2:

Mr. Secretive: The significance of transparency and trust in a relationship

Mr. Secretive is an individual who flourishes when it comes to deception during a relationship and has a remarkable ability to establish and preserve a complex network of secrets, effectively masking his genuine intentions from those close to him. Presented with inquiries, he displays the quintessential behaviors of a consummate pathological liar, demonstrating unparalleled skills in maintaining confidentiality. Indeed, his closet is so crowded with skeletons that it could double as a haunted house designed to spook and thrill. This man is determined to any extent to safeguard his secrets, sparing no effort in concealing his tracks. Anyone entangled with him should exercise extreme caution as Mr. Secretive preys on the unawareness of his intimate partners, manipulating their trust. At the same time, he skillfully conceals the deeds he commits under the shroud of darkness. His life outside the spotlight is conducted with orchestrated moves intended to make his shady deeds invisible to you. He hides behind a persona of charm and respectability; he thrives in plain sight, carefully manipulating every aspect of his life to avoid detection. Whether falsifying stories or fabricating emotions, he has the art of illusion, deceiving those he claims to love and himself. The unfortunate truth is, for Mr. Secretive, the masquerade never ends, and neither does the relentless pursuit to maintain the illusion that is his life.

Recognizing Signs: Mr. Secretive Playbook

The Phone Flipper: Mr. Secretive possesses a peculiar habit of keeping his phone flipped over or facing down. Whenever you catch a glimpse of his screen, he quickly snatches it away, claiming it's a mere habit. But why the secrecy? What is he hiding behind that digital barricade? *Example:* You innocently reach for his phone to check the time, only to witness a flurry of panic as he snatches it away and exclaims, "Oops, sorry! Old habits die hard, you know?"

Social Media Vagueness: Online presence? Ha! He won't post or tag locations or events, and his relationship status is always shrouded in mystery. *Example:* When Brittany confronts Adam about why he never posted pictures together, he casually shrugs it off, claiming he wants to keep things "private." But what's he hiding behind that digital smokescreen?

The Defensive Strategist: Whenever you muster the courage to ask Mr. Secretive about his actions or intentions, he skillfully dodges, deflects, and becomes increasingly defensive. It's as if every question attacks his fortress of lies, and he won't allow a crack to appear. *Example:* You inquire about the female name you spotted on his contact list, and suddenly, he accuses you of invading his privacy or being overly jealous. It's like he's guarding his fortress of lies and won't let you get anywhere close to the truth.

The Shadow App Connoisseur: You might spot a suspicious app icon on his phone, but don't be fooled. He wields shadow apps with dexterity, keeping his secret side ventures securely tucked away from prying eyes. *Example:* You stumble upon an unfamiliar app icon on his phone, but when you ask innocently about its purpose, he brushes it off as a "useless app" or a game he downloaded but never played. You sense a whiff of deceit in the air, but you can't quite put your finger on it.

The Friends and Family Phantom: Despite being in a relationship, Mr. Secretive keeps his partner isolated from his social circle and family. There's always a reason why you never meet his friends or family or join him on holiday visits. He prefers to keep you compartmentalized and away from potential sources that might expose the truth. *Example:* You've been dating for a year, but he always has an excuse when it comes to introducing you to his friends or family. He might claim his friends are too busy or his family lives far away, but as time passes, you start questioning whether you're in a real relationship.

The Identity Concealer: Mr. Secretive takes excellent care to ensure his side chicks remain shrouded in anonymity. You'll find misleading descriptions in his phone contacts like "Dana from work" or "Mom's friend" to conceal their true identities. It's a web of deception, woven meticulously to maintain his double life. *Example:* Curiosity gets the better of you, and you decide to call "Mom's friend" just to say hello. Much to your surprise, the voice on the other end of the line definitely doesn't belong to a mom's friend.

The Outdoor Phone Conversationalist: Mr. Secretive habitually takes his calls outside, away from prying ears. Even in the comfort of his own home, he seeks refuge in the outdoors to ensure his conversations remain shrouded in secrecy. ***Example:*** You're enjoying a cozy evening together, and his phone rings. Without missing a beat, he excuses himself to take the call outside. You watch as he steps onto the patio, his phone pressed to his ear, and a sense of unease settles in. What could he be discussing that requires such secrecy?

Pause for a moment and ask yourself:

1. Have you noticed any changes in your partner's behavior, such as being excessively guarded about their phone?
2. Has he given you reasons to trust him, or have you caught him lying or being deceptive?
3. What are the signs of a secretive person you might have overlooked in past relationships?
4. How can you be more vigilant about identifying these signs in the future?

Now that we have defined Mr. Secretive and some of the tactics he uses, let me share an example of the dangers of getting involved with this kind of man.

The risks of dating Mr. Secretive

Let me introduce you to Eric, the master of secrets and a real charmer. He's got this long-term thing going on with Megan, who's educated, caring, and pretty much an overall catch. Their relationship has its ups and downs, but there's hope. Now, here's the kicker: Eric can't seem to shake off his old shady habits despite having a good woman in his life. He's got not one, but two women, Ari and Lisa, on the side at different points in their relationship. With her intuition on high alert, Megan senses Eric's shady behavior but fails to question it. Meanwhile, Ari becomes Eric's hidden, frisky companion. The two met a year or so before he was in a relationship with Megan. He and Ari would travel to see each other often to hook up. These two used to rendezvous like nobody's business, indulging all weekend long. Despite their good times, Eric and Ari eventually lose contact due to personal issues.

Now, here's where fate does its thing. Eric stumbles upon Ari's picture on social media and hits the like button, setting off a chain reaction of secret conversations. They started innocently reminiscing about old times but then drifted into flirtation, ultimately exchanging nude pictures with plans to see each other. Ari has no clue that Eric's in a serious relationship, and she couldn't care less. Her focus is on hooking up, and Megan, the poor girl, remains blissfully unaware of the whole circus. As Eric continues speaking with Ari, he turns into Mr. Secretive, guarding his phone like it's Fort Knox, flipping it face down, and putting it on silent at all times. He even pulls out a secret agent move—buying a second phone and keeping it hidden in the trunk—because he believes it's the last place he thinks Megan will look.

One day, while Eric was in the shower, Ari did the unthinkable and sent a message to his main phone since he didn't answer the hidden one, but Megan intercepted it. Bam! Furious and hurt as she dives deeper into the inbox, scrolling and uncovering all the explicit messages, sexting, and whatnot. The truth had finally come to light between Ari and Eric. Keeping her anger at bay, Megan watched as Eric came out of the shower, dressed, and left for work before she called Ari to confront her. Now, here's where it gets intense. Megan confronts Ari on the phone, demanding answers and trying to figure out why Eric would pull this crap after she treated him like royalty. But Ari, in her nonchalant swag, just brushes her off, saying Eric isn't her man and what they have going on over there isn't any of her business. Then, she bluntly tells Megan not to call her again. Cold, right? So, Megan unloads all the screenshots and exposes Eric's deceit when he returns home. And man, this dude can't even own up to it, deflecting like his life depends on it. But the pain Megan's feeling isn't a joke, and the relationship? Yeah, it hits rock bottom. Megan kicks him out, and they go months without talking.

About two months go by, and you'd think Eric would take some time off and maybe do some soul-searching, but nope. He's right back at it, swiping through dating apps like he wasn't just in a relationship a month ago. Then he meets Lisa, a free spirit with undeniable chemistry with Eric. They hook up left, right, and center in the first week of meetings. And guess what? During this time, Eric's trying to weasel his way back into Megan's life during the separation, but she's still trying to figure things out, so she's playing the ignore game. But wait for it; here comes the twist. Familiarity drew her back into Eric's web of deceit, and she fell for Eric's charm, and they started talking again. She even invites him to church! But little does she know that while they're spending more time together, he fails to mention Lisa and continues his hidden affair with both women (the guy can't get enough). While Eric and Megan are out on a date, she spots Lisa's name flashing on Eric's phone and asks, "Who's that?" Eric brushes it off as if Lisa is a nobody, just a fling from when they were separated. Unbeknownst to Megan, Eric keeps secrets and can't resist Lisa's allure, even setting up plans for her to come to his place the upcoming weekend.

The following weekend, on the second day after Lisa arrived, Megan hadn't heard from Eric in a couple of days and decided to surprise him at his place after work. When she got there, Eric wasn't home. Megan calls him repeatedly and even leaves a note at his door asking why he's ignoring her. When he returns home, Eric finds the note on his door and fears that Megan is nearby and the two might run into each other while Lisa is in town. Eric thinks quickly and conjures up a story about having to go to work early, advising Lisa that they have to cut her visit short. Lisa noticed something was off and realized that Eric was rushing her to leave after all the arrangements had been made to bring her there. She was not a happy camper! While Eric was dropping her off, Megan began to call again. He ignored her calls but was oblivious that her number was bold and bright on his car's dash, allowing Lisa to memorize it. So, after dropping her off, and despite her secretly memorizing Megan's number, she tries to make a move on Eric, asking him why he was in a rush and they should have a "quick session," if you know what I mean. But he declines the offer and runs back home faster than a cat chasing a laser pointer.

Eric finally decides to call Megan back, but it's too little, too late. She's all upset, and rightfully so! Eric does what any skilled liar would do: he spins a tale about his whereabouts and smoothly invites her over for dinner, thinking he will make everything right again. But guess what? During this cozy dinner, Megan's phone rings, and it's from an unknown number. Suspicious? Megan's face goes from relaxed to "I smell something fishy" in seconds. She picks up the call and with laser-like focus, looks Eric dead in the eyes and drops a bombshell: "Oh yeah, he's right here. I'm looking right at him." Eric was shocked by the statement, thinking to himself, "Who would be asking her about him?" Megan maintains eye contact and goes all in on the phone, saying, "Oh, really!? Well, he told me you two weren't like that." Whoa, hold up! She repeats, "You were just here this weekend?" "You and Eric did what?" Megan finally tells him that Lisa is on the phone and sharing everything about their hookups, right down to the nitty-gritty details—sending Megan all the texts, emails, and receipts. Megan was especially hurt once she discovered that Eric slept with both her and Lisa on the same weekend—without protection! Seriously!?! So, there he sits, speechless, as Megan storms out of his apartment in complete distress. She's probably thinking, "Why did I waste my energy on this two-timing man twice? Ugh!" And it's not just heartbreak—he put her health at risk with all those lies and deceit.

Lesson learned, folks: honesty is the best policy, especially regarding matters of the heart. Eric thought he could pull a fast one, but he got caught red-handed and is now facing the consequences of his actions. Play with fire, and you're bound to get burned. Sorry, Eric, you played yourself!

Peep Game: Demanding Honesty and Transparency

As a young man, my mom once caught me in a lie, and she hit me with some wisdom that stuck with me into adulthood. She said, "Boy, you ain't slick. Remember this: What's done in the dark will always come to light." And then she'd recite Luke 12:2–3, which says, "There is nothing concealed that will not be disclosed or hidden that will not be made known." This biblical principle serves as a reminder concerning a potential partner's inability to be honest, upfront, and transparent. Because here's the thing, when dating Mr. Secretive, no matter how clever he thinks he is, his true colors will eventually show. That's why, when they do, believe what you see and don't tolerate lies and secrets. Take Megan, for example. She could have saved herself some trouble if she trusted her gut and questioned Eric's shady behavior from the get-go. Address them head-on, with no fear. Ignoring them could cost you more than just wasted time. To help you counteract secretive behavior, here are some practical techniques to try:

- **Trust your instincts:** Listen to your gut feelings and intuition when something feels off or suspicious about the person you're dating. Take note of any red flags or inconsistencies in their behavior. *Try This:* If you sense something is amiss, don't dismiss it. Give yourself time to observe and reflect on the situation before making any major decisions.

- **Verify information**: Don't hesitate to verify information independently if you suspect your partner is being secretive or dishonest. Use online resources and social media to cross-check his claims. *Try This:* Conduct discrete online searches and utilize available tools to validate information about your partner if you have doubts.

- **Communicate openly and set expectations**: Establish clear communication from the beginning of the relationship. Express your desire for honesty and openness, and discuss your boundaries regarding cheating. *Try This:* Have an honest conversation with your partner about your expectations for honesty and loyalty.

- **Observe consistency:** Pay attention to your partner's actions and consistency in their words and behaviors. Consistency is a sign of trustworthiness. *Try This:* Take note of the differences between what your partner says and what they do. Address these discrepancies openly and honestly.

Transparency, open communication, and mutual trust are the keys to dodging Mr. Secretive and finding a solid relationship. These are the foundations, no doubt. You must keep your eyes peeled for any inconsistencies in their stories, watch their body language, and see how defensive they get when you ask real questions. It's all about that intuition. Be bold, ask the tough questions, dig deep, and stay aware. That way, you'll avoid falling for Mr. Secretive and create a healthy, fulfilling connection built on honesty and trust. Keep it real, and you'll find the right one. No cap!

Chapter 3:

Mr. Aimless: Understanding the impact of aimlessness in a relationship

I want us to be super clear on who we're talking about. Mr. Aimless, who doesn't have a strong work ethic or clear goals. His only dream is daydreaming about owning a yacht one day, but he has yet to do anything to make this happen. You know the type, right? If you asked him about his plans, he would shrug and say he's living day by day—not thinking about what's next. This way of living won't help anyone succeed, including the women who decide to date a man like him. He might initially look like a good guy but don't be fooled. Behind that nice front, he's just wandering without purpose, going wherever life takes him, without any real goals, plans, or determination to choose a path for himself. Mr. Aimless keeps floating from one forgettable event to another, never really failing but never quite satisfied. He's like a leaf flowing in a stream, occasionally pushed around by what others decide. In a big way, Mr. Aimless believes that being free means not having commitments or responsibilities.

But this kind of total freedom traps him as much as a cage. If you never choose 'where' to be or 'who' to be, you end up lost, as 'anywhere' and 'anyone.' By not standing out, Mr. Aimless becomes invisible in the crowd he creates. Mr. Aimless' life is ruled by chance and what others do. He hops from one interest to another and becomes the perfect picture of someone just going through the motions, watching life pass by instead of living it. Untouched by anything, this numb existence highlights a sad truth: the less he commits to it, the more trapped he becomes by everything.

Recognizing The Signs: Identifying signs of a man without direction or goals.

Dating Mr. Aimless is like trying to build a sandcastle in a storm—doomed from the get-go. Sis, you deserve better than a guy with no roadmap for life and can only offer you a good time. You want a partner who knows what he wants and has a track record of achieving what he sets out to do. Someone who can lead even when the waters get rough. Let's break down some signs and traits to see if you're possibly dating "Mr. Aimless.":

Lack of Leadership Skills: Leading isn't about being a control freak or bossing folks around; it's about inspiring and guiding others. But Mr. Aimless struggles in this area; he can't lead himself, let alone a potential partner. ***Example:*** When it's time to make decisions, he refuses to take charge, saying, "I'm not sure; whatever you want is fine with me." He can't even decide between pizza or tacos; how will he lead you anywhere?

No Marketable Skills: Being a good partner means contributing to the relationship, which means financially as well. It's like, professionally, Mr. Aimless is stuck in beginner mode, unable to find his way to becoming an expert at anything. *Example:* Mr. Aimless is cool working dead-end jobs that barely pay the bills, and he never considers upgrading his skills for better opportunities. Nobody got time to play catch-up with him.

No Goals/Plan: Goal setting is the GPS of life. It gives us direction and purpose. A ship without a route will never reach its destination. Likewise, Mr. Aimless has no roadmap for life and is content to wander, which shows in his lack of goal-setting. *Example:* He's been talking about starting his own business for years, but all he has is a bunch of half-baked schemes and, more importantly, no concrete business plan.

Life is a party: Mr. Aimless is all about the club scene; he treats life like a never-ending party, constantly escaping reality to avoid facing life's challenges and responsibilities. *Example:* When life gets real, he'd instead get drunk, smoke weed, or hang out in the club all weekend. But trust me, real-life problems don't disappear on the dance floor.

Lack of Discipline: Mr. Aimless lacks the self-discipline needed to stick to commitments and follow through on his word. He talks the talk but never walks the walk. *Example:* He promises to hit the gym and start eating healthy, but it's back to his cozy couch and Netflix after a few days. It's like he's allergic to commitment, even to the little things, and sis, you deserve someone who sticks to their word like glue.

Financial Instability: Poor money management and reckless spending are indicators of an aimless attitude toward life. Making it challenging for Mr. Aimless to be a reliable partner. *Example:* He refuses to repair his credit, create a monthly budget, or set up a savings account to invest in the future. Instead, he lives paycheck-to-paycheck, spending carelessly.

Pause for a moment and ask yourself:

1. How do you think dating someone without a clear sense of direction could impact your goals and emotional well-being?

2. How do you balance the desire for a thrilling relationship with the need for a partner who can provide stability for the long term?

3. Have you ever met a guy who is sweet but seems to lack any real direction in life? How did that make you feel?

4. Picture your ideal partner. How important is it for him to have a vision and goals for his life?

Consequences of Getting involved with an Aimless Man

Love might be blind, but it shouldn't be delusional. Don't get me wrong, everyone deserves an exciting or thrilling relationship, but trying to build something solid on quicksand is not the way to go. We've all been there—that moment when you're vibing with someone, sharing laughs, enjoying each other's company. But deep down, you start to wonder: Is this even going anywhere? Are we on the road to something promising or just cruising to a dead end? Before you find yourself trapped with a guy like this, let's dive deep into the potential consequences of dating Mr. Aimless.

Picture this: You're a driven, dynamic young woman with big dreams and bigger goals. You're out here hustling, chasing after your passions, doing you. Then, you stumble upon Mr. Aimless. Sure, he's handsome, fun to be around, and may even seem like a good guy. But here's the scoop: 99% of men like Mr. Aimless have no clear vision for themselves; they have self-identity issues, their finances are always a mess, and they don't know how to lead in a relationship or any aspect of life. He's got dreams and aspirations that change faster than the latest fashion trends. One day, he's all about starting a business, and the next, he's on to becoming a world-renowned DJ. Sure, it's good to have dreams, but when he's flip-flopping like a fish out of water, he's just throwing spaghetti at the wall and hoping something sticks. No man is perfect, and you must start somewhere. We all love a dude trying his best to make it, even if he's caught in a tough spot. It's inspiring when a man is grinding towards a better opportunity, showing steady progress as he puts in the sweat and tears. But then there's Mr. Aimless, chillin' on the couch, waiting for lady luck or you to drop a blessing in his lap. Be warned: if you're trying to hold down a relationship with a dude who's perpetually lost, brace yourself for failure. Some of you have heard the saying, "Stand by your man." Honestly, it's a saying that I somewhat agree with, but only to a degree. It should be more like "Stand by your man only if he has a plan."

Take my own story, for example. Back in the day, I and my now-wife were in the early days of our love journey—just six months deep, to be exact. I had this chance to transition from my job as a hospital security guard to a new opportunity with the city's water department. Talk about a switch-up! Now, I'm not gonna lie; things got rocky—I mean, the learning curve was steeper than a roller coaster drop. I took that risk, pushed myself, and gave it my all. But guess what? A few days shy of completing my probation, I got the boot. Ouch, right? But did I crumble? Nah, I rose like a phoenix from the ashes, and I gave my girl a call. And brace yourself for this—I straight-up told her she should bounce and leave me in the dust because at the time, she was in grad school taking difficult classes, and I didn't want to weigh her down. Now, here's where it gets real. Instead of jumping ship like I encouraged her, she paused and said, "So what's your plan, though?" Surprised by her response, I laid out what I had planned: I told her I would continue working my hustle on the side, stack up, take some classes for new security certification, and then apply for a better security gig than my last one. Unlike Mr. Aimless, I didn't just yap my lips. I went out there, step by step, and did what I said I would. No wishful thinking, no lounging around—just straight-up hustle. Being in a relationship with an aimless man can have consequences beyond moments of annoyance. When you're invested in someone who's all over the place, it can take a toll on your emotional well-being. You might start questioning your goals and aspirations, wondering if you're better off just floating along like him. Your dreams could take a back seat as you try to support and fix his rollercoaster journey. It's not about judging someone's choices, but when his choices start impacting your peace, happiness, and potential, it's time to think it over.

Peep Game: Blindly Following the Blind

I know you're out there, searching for that special someone who'll make your heart skip a beat. And yeah, it's tempting to fall for the flashy ones with their passing charm and alluring charisma. I mean, who doesn't love a good time, right? But avoid getting caught in the trap of temporary thrills because more is needed to build a solid relationship. It's like that ancient wisdom from Matthew 15:14 that says, "If the blind lead the blind, both will end up in the ditch." That might sound a bit old-school, but let me break it down into how this principle applies to dating. Blindly following a man who doesn't know who he is or where he's headed is a recipe for disaster. You need someone with direction, a vision for the future, and, more importantly, a plan to make it happen. At all costs, you should avoid following someone who's lost themselves, or worse, leading you into a ditch of disappointment. It's all about foresight, sis. You should try aiming for a partner who can see beyond the momentary fun and into the long-term potential. Because without that vision, you're both bound to end up unfulfilled and wondering what went wrong. He might seem fun initially, but once the initial excitement wears off, you'll realize that this guy is all flash and has no substance. Here are a few steps to help you avoid the pitfalls of dating "Mr. Aimless.":

- **Consider His Circle of Influence:** Take note of the people he associates with. Ambitious, focused men often seek out like-minded individuals who inspire and motivate them. If his friends lack ambition and direction, it may indicate a similar mindset. *Try This:* When you first meet someone, try to confirm who he spends the most time with. If most of his friends have unstable jobs, show little interest in self-improvement, and are content with living without clear goals, run for the hills.

- **Look for Passion and Interests:** A man with ambition often has passions, hobbies, or interests he actively pursues. Such pursuits indicate a sense of purpose and drive. *Try This:* Share your passions and encourage him to discuss his interests. Evaluate whether he shows enthusiasm and dedication to a personal passion.

- **Assess his long-term goals:** Before committing to a relationship, engage in open and honest conversations about each other's aspirations and plans for the future. Gauge his level of ambition and direction. *Try This:* Ask him about his career and life goals and how he plans to achieve them. If he shows little interest in personal growth or seems content with his current situation, take it as a warning sign.

- **Observe his work ethic:** Pay attention to how he handles responsibilities at work and in his personal life. A lack of motivation and discipline can be indicative of a larger issue. *Try This:* Plan a project or basic activity together and watch how he handles it. He might not have a strong work ethic if he often resists taking initiative or displays little dedication.

- **Evaluate his financial responsibility:** Take notice of his spending habits and approach to financial planning. Irresponsible spending and a carefree attitude can lead to future problems. *Try This:* Discuss financial goals and a personal budget. It could be a red flag if he dismisses the idea or is unwilling to contribute to responsible financial planning.

Please don't fool yourself into thinking you can transform a guy and be the one to give him direction and meaning in life. Warning! You cannot change someone who refuses to change for himself! Sis, a fulfilling relationship is about having each other's backs, cheering on your partner's dreams, and creating a shared vision for an awesome future together. You want a true partner who's got his act together, knows where he's headed, and can lead the way. So peep game, be savvy, and don't settle for entertaining surface-level companionship. Look for someone with the whole package: charm, charisma, and the wisdom to back it up with a clear plan. Life's too short to waste time with someone unsure. Hold out for someone who can take you to new heights and share a fulfilling existence. Keep your eyes open and your heart ready for the real deal. Look, sis.

Chapter 4:

Mr. Hobosexual: Beware the Freeloading Lover

E ncountering exciting people in the dating scene is common. Some bring drama and excitement, and some...
well, their own personal U-Haul ready to move into
your life. Literally. His name is Mr. Hobosexual. Now, you might
be asking yourself, "What on earth is a hobosexual?" According
to the urban dictionary, a hobosexual is a person who jumps
into relationships to have a place to crash. You read it right; this
sly devil will use sex, charm, and deception to gain access to your
life. His underlying desire is a cozy place to call home—your
home. He might casually say he's in between residences or had a
recent unexpected setback. Another strategy is to use emotionally charged stories, such as tales of a challenging childhood,
heartbreaks from previous relationships, or how he feels lost and
alone in the world. As a result, you could feel moved to put on
a cape to act as his rescuer and provide him with the love he
claims he has never had. Don't be fooled; Mr. Hobosexual has a
unique talent for finessing into a comfortable living situation.
Call it survival instincts or downright laziness, but Mr. Hobosexual always looks for the next victim to take advantage of.

Recognizing The Signs: Mr. Hobosexual's Playbook

It's time to put on your detective glasses now, ladies, because we will identify some warning signs to look out for:

The Guilt Tripper: When you start to catch on to his game, Mr. Hobosexual will switch tactics and try to guilt-trip you into letting him stay. He'll act hurt and wounded and play the victim card to make you feel bad for questioning his intentions. *Example:* You confront him about his shacking-up tendencies, and he'll drop lines like, "Wow, I thought you were different" or "I can't believe you don't trust me," just to make you feel guilty for questioning his living situation.

The Permanent/Temporary Houseguest: In the beginning, it all starts innocently enough. Mr. Hobosexual spends the night at your place after a delightful evening together. You might think it's just a casual sleepover, but it's the first step in his master plan to become a permanent fixture in your life. *Example:* He'll come up with reasons to extend his stay. After a few dates, he asked if he could stay at your place because he had a work emergency and didn't want to drive home late. It seemed like a one-time thing, but soon, his toothbrush and extra clothes made their way into your bathroom.

Overly Eager to Move In: Mr. Hobosexual will quickly talk about living together, even before you've had the chance to learn each other's middle names. He's ready to share your address but not your life's responsibilities. *Example:* After just two weeks of dating, Michael started dropping hints about how great it would be to live together. It felt like he was more interested in the apartment than you.

Pause for a moment and ask yourself:

1. Have you ever met someone who seemed to move too quickly in a relationship, professing their love after just a few weeks?

2. What's your take on someone overly eager to move in after a short dating period? Would you find it flattering or concerning?

3. Can you recall a situation where someone you were dating tried to guilt-trip you into letting them stay, and how did you handle it?

4. What steps do you take to ensure your home remains a sacred space, not just a convenient crash pad for someone you're dating?

Allow me to paint you a vivid picture of how this man operates in a relationship.

From Suave to Squatter

Here we have Wayne. He has looks, designer drip, and a personality that draws women in like moths to a flame. He uses material things to make himself appear as the ideal catch for any woman. But beneath that attractive exterior lurked the notorious hobosexual. Wayne's living situation is as stable as a circus clown on a unicycle. He's jumped from baby momma's couch to his cousin's basement, from a temporary sublease to a generous aunt's spare room. He had never truly known the comfort of a place he could call his own. Instead, he relies on the hospitality of others or potential lovers, using his charm and wit to remain welcomed for as long as possible. As if this wasn't alarming enough, it's like he's got this superpower of zeroing in on women with low self-esteem and their place. He's got Sarah in his sights, a sweet soul who's had her share of heartaches in the past. After a brief meeting, Wayne knew she was primed for his game. She seemed like an easy target with her gentle demeanor and desire to be loved. So, Wayne's playbook, like most hobosexuals, isn't rocket science. It's simple—so simple that it often goes unnoticed. He seeks out women like Sarah, who might be lonely or too trusting to exploit their vulnerabilities. He does this by using sex and companionship as weapons to tighten his emotional hold on her. He's all about playing the role of the perfect boyfriend, pouring on affection, and making Sarah think they're soulmates. He's pulling out all the stops; he wines and dines her while plotting how quickly he can move into her life—and, more importantly, her crib.

Another part of his game is to go above and beyond to make himself appear essential. For instance, he ran errands for her, did work around the house, took her car to get washed, etc., without being asked to do so. Sarah thought Wayne was being sweet and genuine with these gestures, but all he was doing was finding reasons to extend his stay at her place a little longer. Sneaky, right? Before she knew it, he casually mentioned how amazing her place was and how wonderful it would be if they could spend more time together under the same roof. After staying just a few nights at Sarah's place, Wayne has all his toiletries in her bathroom and a few drawers in her dresser. Mentally and physically, he's moving in and setting up shop without her even catching on. Soon, Sarah begins to get those gut feelings, but she's shrugging them off, letting Wayne take over her space without any pushback. Her once-peaceful home is starting to feel cramped and claustrophobic. Her BFF, Tammy, is no fool and has noticed a change in Sarah since she started dating Wayne. She couldn't stay silent any longer, telling her, "Girl, take your life back from this puppet master." "Don't let someone else manipulate your emotions and make you feel responsible for taking care of them." Sarah takes Tammy's advice and tries confronting Wayne concerning his living situation. But here's where Wayne plays his next card and diverts her attention by dropping the "L" bomb, confessing his love for her just a few weeks into the relationship. He tells Sarah how he's head over heels and has never felt like this about anyone before. It's a trick to distract her from the whole living-on-her-dime situation. Under the pressure of his alleged feelings, Sarah felt torn between wanting to believe in love and trying to avoid being hurt again. But with a little passion and affection from Wayne, she allows her low self-esteem to cloud her judgment. She starts convincing herself that she has found true love, ignoring Tammy's warning and the bright, lurking red flags. They continued their relationship, and Wayne moved in, kicking back rent-free living on her dime. Wayne kept the facade up for as long as he could, and like clockwork, when things started going south, she reached her breaking point, and he wore out his welcome. At this point, Wayne had already started lining up his next target on his list. When it comes to talking to multiple women, men like Wayne, aka Mr. Hobosexual, must always have plans A, B, C, and D in their back pockets because their living situation depends on them. He will continue his twisted cycle performed with finesse, leaving a trail of broken hearts behind him.

Peep Game: Guard Your Heart

Proverbs 4:23 says, "Above all else, guard your heart, for it is the source of everything you do." For women dating, in order to avoid being seen only as an object or choosing a bad partner that wastes your time, this piece of wisdom is beneficial. It suggests that you should prioritize your emotional well-being and consider your romantic choices carefully. By following this advice, a woman can make wiser choices that keep her safe from harmful relationships and abusive men. The idea of "guarding your heart" has many parts. It's not about closing yourself off from love but about being wise and looking deeper than immediate attractions. This involves creating and following your rules, quickly noticing warning signs, and understanding your value. By being careful like this, you can build a solid basis for a good relationship with respect and true connection instead of just passing emotions or shallow features. It means realizing that not every crush needs to be pursued and that real love is okay to wait for. You've just been given a backstage pass to the playbook of the elusive hobosexual, a character who's mastered the art of using charm and sex to land himself a cozy spot under a trusting soul's roof. The takeaway here is this: His way of life depends on the generosity and naivety of women to provide him with a place to stay. If you've been nodding along as you read, recognizing a little too much of Wayne's shadowy tactics in the person you're with or who's trying to get with you, it's time to pull out your self-love armor and steer clear of these hobosexual types. Your home is your haven, not a hotel. You deserve better than a man who thrives on using emotional manipulation for free rent.

Let's examine some steps to help you avoid these tricksters like Wayne:

Observe His Independence: Pay attention and confirm if he lives independently. Does he have a stable living situation? Does he take responsibility for covering his living expenses? Someone who can manage their life's responsibilities is more likely to contribute to a relationship positively. *Example:* When you meet someone during those initial convos, you need to confirm whether he has a stable living situation that shows he's self-sufficient and not a man looking for someone to take care of him.

Keep Your Home a Fortress: Your space is sacred. Don't be in a hurry to have someone move in just because it feels convenient. Ensure he's there for you, not just for the roof over his head. *Example:* He tells you he thinks moving and splitting the bills will benefit both of you. Before agreeing, see how he reacts when you suggest alternate ways for him to find stable housing before considering sharing your space. His reaction will tell you all you need to know to confirm whether or not he's a hobosexual.

Avoid Fast-Track Declarations of Love: Love takes time to grow. You need to experience every person's emotional side (temperament, sadness, etc.) to love them truly. So, when someone drops the "L" bomb too early, it's often a manipulation tactic. Guard your heart! ***Example:*** If a guy professes his undying love just weeks in, kindly appreciate the sentiment, but don't allow him to pressure you into anything and maintain a healthy skepticism.

Boost Your Self-Esteem: Build a strong foundation of self-love and self-worth and cultivate your desired lifestyle. When you value yourself, you're less likely to fall for someone who preys on your insecurities. ***Example:*** If you feel like a particular aspect of the relationship is hindering your self-esteem, have an honest conversation with yourself and your partner to make the necessary adjustments that best serve your mental health and well-being.

Confront with Confidence: Address concerns about his living situation head-on and without fear, seeking clarity, not assumptions. ***Example:*** When a potential partner tries to avoid proving he has a place, he then tries to divert your attention with affection, hold your ground, and insist on discussing important matters.

By following these steps, you're guarding your heart and paving the way for meaningful connections instead of unwelcome roommates. Don't let the Waynes of the world take advantage of your kindness and compassion. It's essential to arm yourselves with self-respect and take heed of the support of friends who've got your back. Remember, a true partner adds value to your life without compromising your space or self-esteem. So, when you hear the whispers of your instincts or your best friend's truthful advice, don't ignore them. With a little awareness and self-love, you can avoid falling into the trap of those who seek to exploit your kindness for their gain.

Chapter 5

Mr. Wolf:
Love in Disguise

You've probably heard the old saying, "Wolf in sheep's clothing," and honestly, when it comes to dating today, no truer words were ever spoken! While you're on your quest for that special someone, you will stumble across a whole spectrum of guys who, at first glance, seem like the real deal—genuine and maybe even potential husband material. But hold up because not all that glitters is gold, and some of these dudes might be wolves in sheep's clothing! Now, where does this whole "wolves in sheep's clothing" thing come from? You might wonder. Well, I was surprised that it's right out of the Good Book. Believe it or not, it mirrors a situation we've all seen in the dating pool. You can find it in Matthew 7:15, which says, "Beware of false prophets. They come to you in sheep's clothing, but inwardly, they are ravenous wolves." Although these verses describe false prophets trying to take advantage of the church at that time, the verse still serves as a warning about individuals who carefully construct personas that appear harmless or well-intentioned but whose true motives are far from pure. It's all about looking at their actions, motives, and lifestyle.

Now, there's nothing new under the sun, but unlike Mr. Dream Seller, these wolves are pros at playing different roles so believably that they can mess with your perception of reality. These guys use convincing gimmicks to catch unprepared hearts off guard. In the context of dating, there are several types of wolves, but we'll look at three different, prominent types that often get overlooked: the Fake Woke Wolf, the Religious Wolf, and the Digital Wolf. Now, let's break down this ancient wisdom and apply it to dating today, where wolves come in all shapes and sizes, wearing different disguises.

Recognizing The Signs: The Three Wolves Playbook

The Fake-Woke Wolf

We'll start with the Fake-Woke Wolf. Now, to all my sapiosexual sisters, this one's a bit tricky, especially if you've got a soft spot for intellectuals. The fake-woke wolf has this unreal ability to make himself seem like the most profound intellectual man in the room. He's read a few books, knows some trending buzzwords, can rattle off the names of all the big shots in the latest social movements, and he's practically made a career out of sharing equality memes on every social media platform known to man. Heck, he might even throw in some talk about chakras, high-energy vibrations, and all that ancient mysticism stuff, making you feel like you're in the presence of a modern-day philosopher. When you peel back the layers, you'll discover he's just using these social issues as a front, a disguise of activism, to impress and possibly sleep with women. Imagine this: You bump into a fake-woke wolf at a social justice gathering, and he's on fire, passionately advocating for equity, inclusion, and making the world a better place. You can't help but be drawn in by his energetic rants and his talk of dedication to these noble causes. You start thinking, "Wow, this guy really gets it." After the event, you exchange contact information, and he reaches out, sharing a thought-provoking article that genuinely makes you ponder. Your conversations have become deep and meaningful, and he seems sincerely interested in creating a brighter future. Slowly, you fall for this seemingly authentic and thoughtful man, and it's not long before your connection takes an intimate turn. As time goes by, you start noticing cracks in his facade. The activism, it turns out, was more of a show than anything else. You discover he doesn't truly care about the social issues he preached about; it was all just a clever ploy to get women like you into his bed. He peels off his activist and intellectual mask, revealing his completely different side. You were captivated by his charm and ideals, only to realize he was another wolf in sheep's clothing.

So, what's the takeaway here? Don't be too quick to fall for an act. Sure, it's easy to get caught up in someone's passionate rant, but take your time to peel back those layers. Ask the tough questions, see if their actions align with their words, and don't be afraid to walk away if you see those cracks in the façade.

Pause for a moment and ask yourself.

1. How can you separate genuine passion for social causes from someone just putting on a show?

2. What are some signs that can help you spot whether his intellectual depth is real or just an act?

3. Have you ever been in a situation where you felt someone was faking their passion or intellect to impress you? How did you handle it?

The Religious Wolf

Now, let's chat about Mr. Religious Wolf, shall we? Faith is beautiful, and when someone wears it on their sleeve, it can be compelling. But be cautious when you encounter a guy who takes it to the next level, using it as a disguise. I'm speaking of the type of guy who casually drops Bible verses out of nowhere but has difficulty having normal conversations, attending every church event religiously (pun intended) with unwavering dedication just to be seen and heard. He goes on and on about wanting a "God-fearing" woman by his side despite remaining single by choice for several years. Sounds great, right? But what you see on the surface doesn't always align spiritually with what he's hiding beneath. He's a unique character who uses a faith-based persona to get closer to women, hoping it leads to something physical. I know it sounds messed up that men will use religion as a means to prey on women, but I've seen it with my own two eyes. At first sight, you might think you've found a like-minded soul— someone who shares your spiritual beliefs. Please don't allow yourself to get caught up in these Religious Wolf's performances.

Let me paint you a scenario that I witnessed, one that I hope no one ever experiences, but it's essential that I speak on it so that you will understand how to avoid such a situation. Imagine you've been attending the same church for a while, and a Religious Wolf catches your eye. He seems devout and is always there with a comforting smile during Sunday service. He approaches you after the service is over. You two talk and exchange social media info. Once you two connect, he's too eager to engage in deep conversations about faith and spirituality. He's attentive and makes you believe you've found someone who truly understands you and your beliefs. Next thing you know, he's showing up at your Bible study group and becoming a regular. But slowly, during your conversations, he starts sounding more and more like the world and less like the faith he claims to possess. Those spirit-filled convos take a turn with him trying to get you alone, and his true intentions become as clear as day. He makes his move and suggests moving your Bible study sessions to a more private, one-on-one setting away from the group. He says, "Hey, I've been thinking we should have our own Bible study sessions since the current one is only once a week. I just feel it will help us focus better on God's word and have a deeper connection; it'll be more intimate, just the two of us." You, being the faithful and trusting soul that you are, agree. And this is where the trap begins to tighten. After a few meetups, you let your guard down, and those intimate, private Bible sessions evolved into something more physical. His intentions were never about connecting with you to help you grow on a spiritual level; he was using religion as a costume to get you to let your guard down so he could sleep with you and get away with it.

It's sad, but guys like these prey on women who may be struggling with their lustful urges and temptations, much like most people who attend church in the hopes of overcoming old bad habits and bettering themselves. So, keep in mind that real men of God are all about honesty, integrity, and respecting a woman's boundaries.

Pause for a moment and ask yourself:

1. Can you recall when someone you dated or were interested in showed signs of using their faith to get closer to you? How did you handle the situation?

2. Have you ever been in a situation where someone tried to isolate you from a group setting to get closer to you? How did you handle it? Reflect on your past experiences.

3. How do you usually distinguish between a person interested in your spiritual growth and one pursuing a more physical connection?

The Digital Wolf

Mr. Digital Wolf is a true master of illusion. He's got this knack for making you believe he's the guy you've been waiting for—living a life that seems ripped straight from the Hollywood Hills. But what you see isn't always what you get. Sure, online, he's flaunting those nice cars and bundles of cash, laced penthouse condo, but it's all part of a well-orchestrated performance.

Imagine this: You're swiping through your dating app, and bam, there's Mr. Digital Wolf's profile, looking like it's lifted from a luxury lifestyle magazine. The first pic? He leaning casually against the latest sports car with that trademark grin. You keep scrolling, and there are snapshots of extravagant vacations in exotic locations, designer threads, and lavish dinners at five star spots. His bio? It reads like he's the CEO of some tech or music empire. I mean, who wouldn't be intrigued, right? So, you guys match, and the conversation kicks off. He's got charisma for days and a wicked sense of humor. Compliments? He's dishing them out like candy, and he's already talking about planning a date that sounds straight from a romance flick—flying you out for rooftop dinner, followed by a moonlit beach stroll. Date night arrives, and he rolls up in some exotic car. The restaurant? Top-notch, good wine flowing freely, and the food? Oh, it's divine. As the night unfolds, Mr. Digital Wolf keeps the charm going. He's dropping witty lines and even hinting at taking you on a romantic island getaway. You can't help but feel special, right? It's like you've struck gold with this guy, and honestly, who can blame you for getting caught up in his phony world of luxury after you've dealt with so many suckers in the past? But sadly, it's all smoke and mirrors. Mr. Digital Wolf's fake luxurious persona has one sole purpose: to get you into bed. He's a manipulator, using materialistic props plus your longing for love and security against you. By the time the night wraps up, you might find yourself in his swanky apartment, thinking you've landed Prince Charming, ready to share all your goodies. But reality smacks you in the face when the sun rises on your magical evening. Weeks pass, and you start noticing the cracks in his glamorous façade. The sports car he picked you up in? Rented for the week and had to be returned. The posh apartment he seduced you into? It's not his own; he's just house-sitting for a buddy who plays professional sports. That extravagant lifestyle he uses for a front? Funded by stolen credit cards and fraud.

Now that you've seen through his act, you might also realize that the charm and charisma that drew you in were just tools in his playbook. He's nothing more than a con artist or scammer, living in his mom's basement, struggling to make rent. The Digital Wolf took advantage of your desire for a man who seems to have it all, crafting a fake image of success and wealth.

Pause for a moment and ask yourself.

1.   What are some warning signs that someone you're dating might be fabricating their wealth on social media?
2.   Have you ever been tempted to let your guard down by someone's flashy online presence? How did you navigate your feelings and perceptions?
3.   Have you ever been in a relationship where materialism played a significant role? How did it impact your connection?
4.   How can you gauge a person's authenticity when their online persona seems too good to be true?

All three wolves are experts at pretending to be your perfect match by using a disguise. Now that we've got Mr. Fake-Woke Wolf, Mr. Religious Wolf, and Mr. Digital Wolf on our radar, let's unpack their toxic traits with real-life examples.

Faking Passion for Social Causes: He might not even fully understand the causes he's championing, but he's all over social media, posting about rallies, signing petitions, etc. But really, he could care less. It's like he's wearing a mask of virtue, hoping it will pay off. *Example:* He talks a big game about social Justice. But when you get to know him better, you realize he's not actively involved in any real way. It's just a ploy to impress you. He uses activism as a front to get closer and, ultimately, intimate.

Fake Deepness: The Woke Wolf engages in a passionate, thought-provoking conversation that leaves you thinking, "Wow, I've finally found someone on my level mentally." *Example:* He might initially come across as a philosopher, discussing profound topics like the meaning of life or something that appears enlightening, etc. You're impressed, and it's totally understandable, but don't be fooled by fancy vocabulary and deep conversations alone. Take your time getting to know him and seeing if he can walk the talk.

Faith Exploiter: He seems like the most devout and spiritually connected person you've ever met. But beware, it's just a front; he uses religion as a disguise to manipulate situations for physical intimacy. *Example:* He tells you, "Let's explore our faith together in a more intimate setting." And while studying the Bible together, his intentions are solely focused on physically taking things to the next level. Don't fall for it.

Lifestyle Fabricator Specialist: He is all about showing off on social media. He's posting pics of luxury cars and dreamy vacations, just like bait on a hook. It's all a scam to lure you in for pleasure, as he's actually living a deceptive life. *Example:* You meet a guy on a dating app after viewing his profile, full of fake pictures of a lavish lifestyle. It's hard not to be drawn to his apparent wealth and luxury. But you soon discover his flashy possessions are all rented or borrowed, and his lifestyle is not as extravagant as he portrays; it's all part of his playbook to manipulate you into bed.

Mirroring Your Values: All three wolves are like chameleons, blending into your world seamlessly. They're pros at mimicking your beliefs and passions, making you feel like you've found your soulmate. *Example:* You're passionate about art and culture. You meet this guy who appears to share your passion. He talks about visiting art galleries, attending poetry readings, and loving everything you adore. It feels like you've found your perfect match, and that connection grows stronger. After being intimate, you learn he doesn't care about art or culture at all. He's just pretending to be into it because he knows that mirroring a woman's values can be used to deceive her into getting intimate.

Peep Game: The Parallels with Jesus' Wisdom

Ladies, when it comes to navigating the complex world of dating and relationships, there's a lesson from the wise words of Jesus that's more relevant today than ever. Picture this: Jesus's warning to people about wolves lurking beneath sheep's clothing might not sound like your typical dating advice. But trust me, the principle he presents is like a beacon guiding us through the stormy seas of modern romance. So, let's break it down and see how Jesus' wisdom can help you steer clear of those who would deceive and use you for their gain. First off, Jesus wasn't just talking about ancient prophets in robes; he was giving us a timeless message about spotting deception. In the dating world, these 'wolves' don't come dressed as literal sheep, but they're experts at putting on a facade. They'll make you feel special and act like the perfect catch. But behind that innocent smile might be a wolf hungry for something entirely different. Jesus is basically saying, "Don't be fooled by appearances." Now, think about it: isn't that something most women have encountered in their dating lives? The guy who says all the right things seems genuine, but he is just looking for a quick fling. It's heartbreaking when you realize that someone you trusted turned out to be a wolf in disguise. That's why, as I mentioned in the earlier chapters, it's crucial for you to stay vigilant, trust your instincts, don't rush into things, and take the time to get to know someone. But here's the cool part: when you apply Jesus' advice and stay true to yourself, you're not just protecting your heart but also ensuring that you attract the kind of person who values you for who you are. Authenticity, intelligence, and being genuine are like a magnetic force, drawing in the right people who appreciate your worth. So, the next time you swipe and match or meet someone giving wolf vibes, remember this timeless wisdom. Be the shepherd of your own heart, and don't let those wolves in sheep's clothing pull the wool over your eyes. Peep game, sis, and most importantly, stay true to yourself. Remember, you're not just another ordinary sheep in the flock. Here are actionable steps that are as unique as you are because you deserve nothing less:

Assess Their Contribution Beyond Dating: People who genuinely care about a cause often seek to make a meaningful impact, regardless of their relationship status. Look for signs that he's involved in these causes, even when he's not trying to impress you. *Example:* See if he continues his activism even after your relationship deepens, demonstrating his passion goes beyond dating.

Respectfully Challenge Their Knowledge: Do a little research, then ask more profound questions about the topics he claims to be passionate about. Authenticity usually withstands scrutiny. *Example:* Ask about his educational background and what field he claims to be an expert in. Look to see if he engages in thoughtful discussions, providing proof to back it up, or if he sounds unsure, just relying on buzzwords and pretending to know what he's talking about.

Get to Know His Intentions: Don't take someone's passion at face value. Dive deeper into their involvement in the causes they champion or the faith they profess. *Example:* Don't rush into deep spiritual conversations with a guy you've just met. Start with casual talks about faith and values. Ask questions like, "What does your faith mean to you?" or "How do you practice your spirituality?" Pay attention to his answers. Be cautious if he consistently steers the conversation toward physical intimacy rather than discussing genuine spiritual growth.

Dig into His Past: Do some detective work on his past relationships. Check if he has a history of using spirituality to manipulate women. If he's got a trail of broken hearts with similar stories, you'll want to steer clear. *Example:* If his exes all say, "He was super spiritual until he got what he wanted," that's a clear warning sign.

Verify Their Social Media Lifestyle vs. Reality: When someone's online presence is flashy and over the top, question whether it matches his real life. *Example: Have a* conversation to discuss the extravagant profile photos he posted and the stories behind them, or gently ask about the source of his wealth to gauge if it's legit work. Usually, if he's a fraud, the story won't add up.

Chapter 6:

Mr. Potential:
The Hope Dealer

We are all works in progress; we have dreams, ambitions, and room for growth. So, it's understandable how most women are attracted to guys who strive to be better and reach for the stars, right? However, Mr. Potential is a different story. So, who is Mr. Potential? Well, he's not Mr. Dream Seller, promising you the moon without any substance to back it up. He's not Mr. Aimless, drifting through life partying, either. Mr. Potential has ideas but no real plan; he might have a history of accomplishments, but he got stuck and fell off somewhere along the way. Maybe he's been procrastinating or has yet to fully realize his potential. Either way, there's a thin line between being a go-getter, utilizing one's potential, and just pure wishful thinking. I'm sure you've probably heard the saying, "Don't fall in love with potential". Yet, sometimes, women find themselves doing exactly that. Mr. Potential is what I call a hope dealer, he's exceptional at making women fall in love with the possibilities, especially when he occasionally shows flashes of the amazing person he could be or perhaps once was. When you meet a guy like this, he'll seem like a diamond in the rough, full of promise, but, and it's a big *but*, he never quite reaches his full potential for whatever reason, whether in his love life or professional goals. Getting involved with a man like Mr. Potential can be incredibly frustrating. Why? Because his habit of putting off the necessary work to achieve personal growth will guarantee a zero return for all the time and energy you invest. It's like pouring all your hard-earned savings into a promising business with potential that never turns a profit—in simple terms, it's a trap. A *hope trap* that a hope dealer has carefully set up. Many women find themselves caught in this web of hope, some even willingly staying in it for years despite the lack of progress in their relationship. Mr. Potential understands that hope can be a powerful force, especially after a woman catches feelings or gets emotionally invested, and then he uses that to his advantage. Now, let's go deeper into Mr. Potential's hope trap to understand why so many women fall for it and, most importantly, how to avoid it.

The Hope Trap: A House Half-Built

The hope trap arises when a woman remains in a dead-end relationship because she believes a guy has the potential to be an ideal partner but ends up waiting for change that never comes. To illustrate better, consider the Hope Trap, the dating equivalent of HGTV's "Fixer Upper" show. But instead of risky home renovations, it's your love life on the line. And starring in this show is Mr. Potential, the guy who's like that half-finished house you couldn't resist and want to fix. You go inside, and at first glance, you see promise, potential, and a bright future. Before you know it, you find yourself daydreaming about transforming this run-down house into the dream home you've always wanted. You're so focused on the "potential" that you overlook the half-painted walls (his unresolved issues), the leaking roof (his emotional baggage), and the shaky foundation (his unproductive habits). You convince yourself, "Once I fix this place, it'll be the best property on the block." This hypothetical daydreaming about repairing the house, aka Mr. Potential with some TLC, produces the illusion that pulls women into his hope trap. In other words, dating Mr. Potential is more than just a work in progress; it's a gamble. He's a forever project—a construction site with no end in sight. Now, I'm not saying you should only date men who are already at the highest level of their careers or have achieved all their dreams. As I mentioned, we all have our journeys and room for growth. I am saying that on your dating journey, you should only give your time to men who are actively pursuing their goals, who are driven to be the best version of themselves, and who are not satisfied with living below their full potential. Men like Mr. Potential should be approached with caution while dating. What sets him apart from the other Misters we've discussed is that he has something going for himself, in other words, potential. Maybe a decent job in a high-demand career field or a valued talent or skill. These types of men possess gifts that are attractive, yet they have a bad habit of falling short of their potential due to a lack of focus or a poor work ethic. Even though their dreams are inspiring to listen to, without a well-thought-out plan and some hustle behind them, these dreams will remain unfulfilled. For instance, he might be an *Entrepreneur with Big Dreams but Always Broke.* He may have impressive business ideas and dreams of financial success, or maybe he's got a ton of potential, but he can't seem to make it profitable. Then there's the *Creative Unemployed Artist,* who crafts beautiful songs, claiming to be on the brink of fame and fortune. However, his financial struggles and several unsuccessful albums and mixtapes raise concerns. Supporting a man's dreams when dating is commendable, but I warn you, don't rely solely on his potential. Be sure he has a concrete plan and is actively working toward success. Women who fall under the influence of Mr. Potential's hope trap find themselves stuck by believing the delusion that their love alone can fix him and inspire him to break free from mediocrity. However, it's a grave mistake because regardless of how strong a woman believes her love is or how promising the potential of a man may appear, he will always be caught in a cycle of struggle if he repeatedly delays achieving his life's goals or constantly chases after the next big thing, taking you on a one-way trip straight to the hope trap. Many women find themselves willingly trapped, even when they know the relationship isn't profitable. They invest precious time attempting to fix a man, hoping he realizes his potential, often neglecting their aspirations and goals. That's why it's vital that I not only expose the behaviors or traits of Mr. Potential but also shine a light on why I believe women fall for his game and think this way when approaching relationships.

The "I Can Fix Him" Syndrome

I want to take a moment and be clear that it's not my goal to bash women or downplay your inherent nurturing nature, nor am I making any excuses for men like Mr. Potential or their contributions to causing women to develop the "I Can Fix Him" syndrome. I believe it's necessary not only to provide Mr. Potential's playbook but also to highlight the mindsets that women may have that Mr. Potential looks to exploit so you can spot and avoid men like him. So, what is the "I Can Fix Him" syndrome? It's a mindset that occurs when a woman has a misguided belief that love, compassion, sex, or support can miraculously transform a loser of a guy, aka Mr. Potential, into the man living to the maximum potential she imagines in her mind. The "I Can Fix Him" syndrome is one of the oldest and most frequently used dating philosophies because, in my opinion, women are natural nurturers. Most men, including Mr. Potential, know this and take advantage of this innocent feature. This nurturing approach often leads some women to fall into the hope trap without fail. In essence, women who date with the "I Can Fix Him" syndrome take on the role of architects; they see themselves as personally responsible for ensuring their men's success on every level. The only problem is that completing such a task is like trying to turn a half-built trap house into a 10-bedroom beachfront mansion. Not gonna happen!

For example, take Kim and James. Kim is a woman with a huge heart and has no idea she was suffering from the "I Can Fix Him" syndrome. She stumbles upon James, a man with undeniable potential who dreams of climbing the corporate ladder but has a job-hopping habit and a poor track record regarding money management. Kim was optimistic despite James's obvious issues, and the two began dating. During that time, James showed glimpses of his potential but made no real progress towards his goals. All the while, Kim was too focused on imagining all the ways she could "fix" James and create a future where they'd both thrive together, sharing their success and happiness. Now, let's take a moment to unpack this. James, with all his potential, can't seem to hold down a job or make wise financial decisions. Since they've been together, it seems like every time he took a step forward, he'd make some poor choices and end up taking two steps back. He demonstrates a reckless disregard for his paycheck, as if it were a hot potato, discarding it without hesitation upon its contact with his hands. But Kim, bless her soul, continued to invest her time and energy into trying to "fix" James. Offering to help him with budgeting to manage his finances better, she sent him links to motivational talks and books to read; she even revamped his resume to make him more desirable to better employers. She convinced herself that providing her unwavering support and encouragement would magically transform James into a responsible, financially savvy partner. The problem was that James didn't get the memo and remained as inconsistent as ever. It became apparent that James wasn't following the script Kim had written in her mind. This led to frustration and resentment on both sides and their relationship began to suffer. Even with the best intentions, Kim couldn't motivate James to change. She discovered that no amount of encouragement or support could light a fire under him if he didn't want it for himself. The combination of the following two traits contributed to Kim's mindset and her development of the "I Can Fix Him" syndrome. The first was her *delusional belief in her transformative power,* and the second was her *emotional invest-ment attachment issues.*

Firstly, Kim's delusional belief in transformative power is rooted in her natural desire to assist and nurture. But, her extreme confidence in this ability or transformative power comes from her imagination. Her belief was so strong that it caused her to ignore the reality of James' self-destructive habits and actions. It's unfortunate, but Kim got played by James, aka Mr. Potential, because she allowed her intense optimism about his potential to fuel her delusional belief in her transformative power. In other words, Kim set herself up for failure by believing that her influence over James would inspire him to become the finished product she imagined in her head. Without a doubt, I'm more than sure Kim's love and support would offer infinite value to improving his situation if given to the proper guy. But she forgot that the primary rule when dating a man with potential is never to take personal responsibility for advancing his situation; that's on him! He must make the final decision to step up and start living a life of purpose instead of potential. Don't be like Kim, who let her delusional belief in transformative power deceive her into believing that she could get James or any man to become more than what he desired for himself.

The second characteristic that led to Kim developing the I Can Fix Him" syndrome is her irrational fear of losing her emotional investment. This way of thinking took shape after Kim caught feelings and developed a strong emotional attachment to James. Even though James was an unproductive partner, Kim let her irrational fear of losing what she invested (time, emotions, energy, and money) in her relationship with James. Kim's irrational fear of losing her emotional investment caused her to prolong a doomed relationship with James much past its prime because the fear of cutting her losses seemed too difficult. It's common for women with Kim's thought process to believe that quitting a relationship would mean losing everything. The fear and anxiety Kim experienced kept her stuck in James's hope trap, jeopardizing her growth and happiness for zero return.

The key signs that you are dating or in a relationship and have the "I Can Fix Him" syndrome are when you have an overwhelming emotional attachment to your partner and an unhealthy desire to help him reach his goals even when he's not meeting your needs or living up to his potential. You find yourself deeply invested, often feeling like your happiness depends solely on their success in life. You might create excuses for their shortcomings, making it difficult to see the reality of the relationship and when it's time to move on. If the following signs describe how you approach dating or relationships, I suggest taking time for some self-reflection and re-evaluating your priorities. Addressing these patterns and emotions head-on is essential for you to avoid developing the "I Can Fix Him" syndrome or finding yourself stuck in a hope trap with Mr. Potential. That's why it's crucial to make sure that you don't let your fear of losing your emotional investment in Mr. Potential or any other guy prevent you from finding healthy connections that correspond to your best interests when dating or in a relationship.

Pause for a moment and ask yourself.

1. Have I dated someone with potential who has never quite lived up to it? How did that make you feel, and what did you learn from it?

2. Moving forward, what steps can you take to build a relationship in which both parties feel pleased and supported?

Peep Game: Purpose Over Potential

We have discussed how women like Kim allow their delusional belief in transformative power and irrational fear of losing their emotional investment to create the "I Can Fix Him" syndrome mindset and how they land themselves in Mr. Potential's hope trap or a dead-end relationship. We also covered the dangers of falling in love with the possibilities of a man's potential instead of the reality of his actions. Now, let's talk about solutions, or, Mr. Purpose! He's got goals, dreams, and a roadmap to get there. When you're dating Mr. Purpose, you're essentially choosing a partner who's already building his empire and has a clear vision for his future. Now, these two fellas, Mr. Potential and Mr. Purpose, might seem similar on the surface, but trust me, they're as different as night and day. That's why learning to spot the difference between Mr. Purpose and Mr. Potential while dating will save you from heartache and disappointment. The next time you find yourself dating and presented with multiple options, try devoting your attention to men like Mr. Purpose, who are determined and know what they want. Men like Mr. Purpose have a clear vision for their goals and are focused on long-term priorities. He's looking for a partner to complement his life, not complicate it. Unlike Mr. Potential, you don't have to attempt to build or fix Mr. Purpose. You'll feel a sense of stability and security when you're with him. He's responsible and dependable, and can balance his personal life with his ambitions. This guy may not have the flashy charm of Mr. Potential, but what he brings to the table is far more substantial. So, let's examine in more detail what differs between dating Mr. Purpose and Mr. Potential.

Mr. Purpose vs. Mr. Potential

It's essential to be honest with yourself about your goals and what you want in a relationship. Because in the end, whether you date Mr. Purpose or Mr. Potential is a choice only you can make or not, sis. It's a choice that can profoundly shape your romantic future, and you deserve to know exactly what you're getting yourself into. Let's break down what these two types of men bring to the table.

1. Vision vs. Dreaming Big

Mr. Purpose: He's the man with a vision and a game plan, and he's actively working on it. He's got his career and life goals, and he knows where he's headed. When you ask him about his future, he's got detailed answers that show he's been thinking about it.

Mr. Potential: This guy dreams big, but his dreams are just that—dreams. He might talk about starting a business or becoming a millionaire, but there's no concrete plan or action behind it. He's still in the *someday, one-day* phase.

Results:

- Dating Mr. Purpose means you're more likely to be with someone who can provide stability and direction in your life. You'll see progress together.

- Dating Mr. Potential can lead to frustration as you wait for him to turn those dreams into reality. It might never happen, and you might find yourself stuck in a stagnant relationship, a.k.a. the hope trap.

2. Consistency vs. Flakiness

Mr. Purpose: He's consistent in his efforts to build a life together. He's dependable, whether it's calling you regularly, setting up date nights, or showing up when he says he will.

Mr. Potential: This guy can be hot or cold and is pretty inconsistent. He might be all in one moment and distant the next. It's like trying to catch smoke with your bare hands—you'll get burned.

Results:

- Dating Mr. Purpose means you can trust him to be there for you, which is essential for a healthy relationship.

- Dating Mr. Potential can lead to confusion and insecurity. You deserve someone who prioritizes you consistently.

3. Action vs. Excuses

Mr. Purpose: He's all about action. When he says he's going to do something, he follows through. If there's a problem, he's solution-oriented, holds himself accountable, and doesn't make excuses.

Mr. Potential: Excuses, excuses, excuses. This guy might have a laundry list of reasons why he can't do things right now. It's like he's allergic to effort and will deflect or become offensive when confronted with why things aren't done like he said they would be.

Results:

- Dating Mr. Purpose means you'll be with someone who can handle challenges and solve problems together. It's a partnership built on action, not empty words.

- Dating Mr. Potential often leads to a dead-end relationship where things don't move forward. You'll find yourself making more compromises than he does.

4. Investment vs. Convenience

Mr. Purpose: He's invested in you emotionally, mentally, and sometimes even financially. He prioritizes your growth and happiness because he sees a future with you.

Mr. Potential: This guy treats every relationship as a convenience. He's there when it's easy for him, but when things get tough, he's quick to bail out or distance himself.

Results:

- Dating Mr. Purpose means you'll experience a deep, meaningful connection where you are both invested in making the relationship mutually beneficial.

- Dating Mr. Potential often leads to heartbreak because he's not fully committed. You deserve someone who's all-in, not just when it's convenient for them.

Remember that it's not about settling but finding a partner who shares your life goals and values. Don't be afraid to be choosy when it comes to your happiness and well-being. Here are five tips to help you avoid dating men like Mr. Potential and make informed decisions on your dating journey.

1. *Examine His Commitment to Self-Improvement:* Ask questions about his self-improvement efforts. Mr. Purpose has an action plan and actively seeks personal growth, while Mr. Potential never prioritizes it.

2. *Dreams vs. Reality:* Compare his dreams to his current daily routine. Mr. Purpose will actively work towards his dreams, whereas Mr. Potential may have big dreams but lack the drive to pursue them.

3. *Handling Setbacks:* Observe his response to setbacks and failures before committing to him. Mr. Purpose remains determined and learns from adversity, whereas Mr. Potential usually has a habit of giving up too easily when life gets tough.

4. ***Time Management Insights:*** Pay attention to his daily
   routine and time management skills. Mr. Purpose will
   have a schedule aligning with his goals, meeting dead-
   lines, and completing work. In contrast, Mr. Potential
   may have a less organized approach to handling his responsibilities, leaving behind several unfinished projects.

Moving forward, don't try to speed up the process and become a do-it-yourself relationship builder, attempting to fix
every man you date. Most importantly, don't deceive yourself
into believing that you can change a man's bad habits with love,
sex, or support. Pay attention to the reality of a man's actions
rather than falling in love with their potential, which might or
might not happen. Instead, focus on developing a balanced,
win-win relationship with guys like Mr. Purpose, where you're
not constantly playing the role of a fixer or savior because a successful relationship is about two individuals coming together,
growing mutually, and enhancing each other's lives. You deserve
a partner already on his path—a man who knows his potential
and is actively working towards it. Choose wisely, and your journey will be filled with purpose and meaning.

Chapter 7:

Mr. Familiar - Using the Past to Win You Over

M r. Familiar is a man who uses the art of familiarity to establish a connection with women from their past that they're interested in sleeping with. His approach is all about hoping his familiar face will be enough to slide into your DMs, then using familiarity to slowly but surely slide his way to your bed. This low-key, overlooked tactic has been successful in helping Mr. Familiar rekindle old connections with ex-lovers or make new ones with women from his past, like a former classmate or co-worker, etc. Another way Mr. Familiar tries to reconnect with women from his past is to use old shared interests, experiences, or memories to create a sense of comfort and gain a woman's trust. Imagine you're scrolling through your social media, and you receive a friend request from a guy you barely remember from school. It's been a long time since you've seen each other, but all of a sudden, he starts messaging you, liking your photos, and sending you funny memes. You might be wondering, "What's really going on?" Even if he still got it and the years have been good to him, be cautious, sis! Just because he remembered how much you loved pepperoni hot pockets and watching 106 and Park back in the day doesn't mean he knows the real you today, and vice versa. In this chapter, we'll expose how Mr. Familiar cleverly uses nostalgia, shared interests, and trust-building convos in his approach to mislead women.

Recognizing the Signs:

Mr. Familiar wants to reconnect to see if he can sleep with you. But before you get caught up in nostalgia mind games, here's the lowdown on how to spot and handle Mr. Familiar:

Curiosity-Piquing Questions: Mr. Familiar uses curiosity-piquing questions as part of his strategy to reconnect with you. He pretends to be genuinely interested in your present circumstances to encourage you to share more details. With this approach, he seeks to develop a deeper connection by taking an active interest in your life. *Example:* He'll ask open-ended questions like, "Where did you decide to go after graduating?" and "What's the most thrilling adventure you've had since moving there?"

The Nostalgic Icebreaker: Mr. Familiar is skilled at leveraging your shared memories to his benefit. He accomplishes this by initiating conversations starting with phrases like "Do you remember when..." and sharing his cherished memories that bring back thoughts of you. He intends to evoke nostalgia and establish a bond based on your common past experiences. *Example:* In one of your discussions, he might say something like, "Hey, do you remember that time when we came close to being caught sneaking into the movies? We ended up cuddling together to avoid being seen by the attendant. "Ahh, it feels like a lifetime ago."

Trust-Building Conversations: Mr. Familiar initiates long phone calls or video chat sessions, hoping to establish a stronger bond and slowly become your go-to confidant. Through these trust-building conversations, he aims to check your boundaries, strengthen your bond, and ultimately gain your trust to arrange potential future dates. *Example:* After several conversations with Mr. Familiar, you begin to lower your defenses and confide in him about your everyday personal life. Now that a foundation of trust has been established, he slowly redirects the conversation by asking when you might be available to spend some alone time together to talk more.

The Inside Joke Card*:* This approach is a clever and playful way Mr. Familiar uses to strengthen a bond or rekindle a connection with someone. He uses inside jokes from the past that only the two of you understand, with the purpose of reintroducing you to your shared connection through laughter and jokes. *Example:* He overhears you purchasing fast food while on the phone and asks, "Hey, Greedy, are you still stealing fries from the bottom of the bag?" You giggle as you recall how you used to take his fries when he wasn't looking and respond, "I plead the fifth." He used this humorous reminder in the hopes of bringing back emotions that make you feel special or let your guard down.

When someone from your past reemerges, it's essential to trust your instincts and maintain boundaries until you can confirm his true motives. Don't let familiarity cloud your judgment. It's essential to read between the lines when dealing with Mr. Familiar.

Pause for a moment and ask yourself:

1. Did someone from the past try to rekindle a connection by making you laugh and reminisce? (Consider whether he's attempting to recreate the closeness you once had.)

2. Is someone from your past who you reconnected with trying to build trust too quickly? Be cautious if he's trying to build trust rapidly through long conversations. Real trust takes time to develop.

3. What's the real reason the ex-boyfriend, former classmate, or co-worker is suddenly interested in reconnecting after all these years? Don't be swayed by nostalgia alone; ask him why he is here, hitting you up.

4. Does he frequently bring up shared memories as conversation starters? Be cautious if he's trying to rekindle connections solely based on the past.

5. Do you know who he has become over the years? Consider whether you know this person's current values, goals, and character. People change over time, not always for the better.

Now that we have gone over some of Mr. Familiar's approaches, I want to share an event that occurred while I was writing this book and how it inspired this chapter, considering the ironic timing. It all began when one of my wife's friends came over to our house for a visit. After exchanging greetings, we engaged in conversation. Curiously, she asked, "How close are you to finishing your masterpiece?" It had been a few months since I mentioned the idea of writing a book to her, so her curiosity was understandable. With a smile, I proudly informed her that the book was almost complete. I expressed my appreciation for her support and contributions to the project. Since we were on the topic, I asked her what was new in her life since our last conversation. She sighed and revealed that she had recently met someone, but things didn't go well. About a month ago, an old college classmate—we will call him Nick for the sake of the story—slid into her DMs. Wondering about his sudden interest, I asked, "Why do you think he decided to reach out all of a sudden?" She replied, explaining that although she barely knew him during their time on campus, he seemed nice, plus they were part of the same social circle of friends. She recounted that his initial message revolved around asking about her living in central FL. He mentioned being there frequently and suggested catching up. Reluctantly, she agreed and dismissed it. She acknowledged that if he hadn't been "familiar," she probably wouldn't have responded to his DM in the first place. Curiosity got me, so I asked what happened next. She revealed that a few days later, she and Nick had a lengthy conversation that lasted six hours. "You must be kidding!" I said. She confirmed they stayed up talking about work and relationships and reminiscing about their shared college experiences. I jokingly remarked, "That wasn't just a conversation but an all-night telethon." Continuing her story, she shared that Nick sent her a spontaneous message a week later, saying he was in town and asking if she was still open to catching up over coffee. She agreed, and their coffee meetup turned into spending the entire day together. It caught her off guard, but she decided to go with it. However, the story takes a turn from here. She explained that after Nick returned home, they continued to talk and even planned a weekend trip together. I interrupted and asked, "Wait a minute, you agreed to a weekend trip after just three weeks of talking?" With a smile, she responded that she knew it was soon. Still, during the trip planning process, she communicated her boundaries, informing Nick that she expected good vibes only with no sexual involvement. He understood and agreed to behave as a complete gentleman. Eager to hear more, I asked, "What happened during the trip?" She shared that they had dinner near the beach, enjoyed the beautiful sights, stayed in an amazing Airbnb, and even shared a kiss. It sounded like a truly wonderful time, I remarked. She agreed but then revealed that, after some drinks, Nick crossed a line later that night. Instead of simply cuddling, he attempted to engage in inappropriate behavior by literally trying to dry hump her at 3 a.m. She had to remind him of the boundaries they had discussed. He backed off, and they continued to enjoy the trip, ending it on a high note, or so she thought.

I asked her if they had spoken since the trip. She shared that Nick had suddenly started cutting their lengthy conversations short once he returned home. Despite the great time they had shared, arranging a second date was not mentioned. I inquired about their most recent conversation, and she admitted that he had ghosted her for a few days before reappearing with excuses about work and needing time to sort out his personal life. I interjected, calling it typical *lame-dude behavior*. Puzzled, she asked, "But why would a guy go through the effort and spend time and money on a beautiful trip just to ghost me? I don't understand," she said. I provided a straightforward answer that caught her off guard: "To sleep with you, sis, that's why!" She couldn't wrap her mind around it and questioned me, "So, he love-bombed me, right?" I clarified that it wasn't exactly love-bombing, which is just excessive flattery or showering you with unneeded or unwanted gifts. I explained how men like Nick used ties with an old circle of friends to improve their chances of avoiding rejections when they approached women. I highlighted Nick's use of curiosity-piquing questions about where she lived to break the ice when he DM'd her the first time. I mentioned how if Nick were a stranger instead of a familiar face, she would have probably curved him instead of answering the DM, let alone giving him her number so soon. She agreed. Also, I pointed out how she let her guard down even more after that six-hour phone session of "trust-building conversations" full of "nostalgic" stories and jokes. I explained how Nick used those convos as a means to get her more open to meeting up later on. She thought about it for a second and agreed. I asked her, "Why do you think he was conveniently in your city for a surprise to pop up immediately after that talk?" Then I reminded her how he lowkey stretched a simple coffee date into an all-day affair. At this point, I can see her slowly connecting the dots in Nick's game. "Keep going," she asked politely with a smirk. Now he has you primed up to test your boundaries because, again, Nick's goal is to sleep with you. That's it. He knows your guard is slightly down from the convos and the coffee date. So, he introduces the idea of a weekend trip to test your level of comfort with being alone with him overnight. Now, despite you being straightforward about your expectations for the weekend, saying no sex, just good vibes in his mind, by agreeing to go and helping with planning for the trip, you're probably open to the possibility of sex. So, he agreed to be a good boy, but he knew he would stick to his plan for the weekend and try you anyway.

Curious about the motivations behind Nick's behavior, she questions why guys like him go to such lengths and put on a façade. I explained that for individuals like Nick, it's easier to invest in "wining and dining" you, arranging a nice beachfront room and treating you like his girlfriend for a weekend than to be honest about their intentions. Whether you kept your boundaries up or gave in and slept with him, his ultimate goal remains the same: to distance himself afterward by using phrases like "needing space" to figure things out. Nick utilizes familiarity and comfort to lower your defenses and try to sleep with you gradually.

I admit that this approach is often underestimated, acknowledging that even I used it successfully in my past dating experiences. That's why it's crucial to prioritize genuine and authentic connections rather than relying solely on familiarity and giving a person from your past the benefit of the doubt. I strongly advise that you base rekindling any old connection on who the person has become today, not the shared old memories from the past. I am glad that she canceled Nick. We continued our conversation, and she graciously thanked me for the valuable insights.

Peep Game: The Delilah Effect

There are plenty of references in the Good Book about people using deceit in relationships to get what they want. Among these complex stories, one particular tale from the Book of Judges comes to mind that highlights the consequences of being lured by a familiar face from the past. The story I'm referring to is Samson and Delilah. If there's ever a story about how someone used a past connection to manipulate a person's desires, this is it. But even though Deliah was no angel, let's not forget that dating is a two-way street. Just like Samson allowed himself to be played by Delilah by willfully ignoring her sketchy behavior patterns, some women dating today are doing the same thing and find themselves suffering the same fate from men like Mr. Familiar.

Delilah didn't just rely on familiarity; she was relentless in her pursuit of his secrets, determined to get him to reveal the source of his strength. Her patience paid off once Samson got too comfortable, lowered his guard, and eventually exposed his weakness to her. And while today's dating scene isn't filled with men looking to expose your physical vulnerabilities, there are plenty of individuals who want to discover your emotional and psychological weaknesses to exploit them for their gain. You see, just like you, Samson had a lot going for himself—strength, charm, and living a purposeful life. But there was one little chink in his armor: his weakness for Delilah. She used something incredibly potent to seduce Samson—their history. Sound familiar? She didn't have to start from scratch; she had a roadmap to his heart. The same thing can happen to women today.

When a man from your past resurfaces, he often knows which buttons to push to get you going. Look, we're all an easy target for the comfort of familiarity. It's like you meet someone, connect, time passes, and then, out of the blue, he reappears, stirring up your emotions until you give in to them. It's like déjà vu all over again, and you can't help but wonder if he's changed or if he's back with the same old song and dance. Samson fell victim to Delilah's mind games because she used their shared history for personal gain. I want to share some lessons from Samson's story to help you avoid falling for Mr. Familiar's games.

Lessons from Samson

Samson's story is more than just ancient folklore; it's a wake-up call that hits close to home. It contains valuable insights that resonate even today. Here are some critical lessons from Samson's story to take away that will help you avoid men like Mr. Familiar.

Lesson 1: Be Wary of Familiar Faces

Similar to the story of Samson, the past can be a tricky and deceptive place. Delilah knew Samson from before, and she popped up like some guys from your past who might resurface and bring back old memories. She consistently applied pressure and used her familiarity to gain access to make Samson feel at ease, causing him to become vulnerable unknowingly. Delilah pretended to be concerned about Samson's well-being while having hidden intentions. When navigating the dating world, it's important to be mindful that not all familiar faces have good intentions. If a man from your past suddenly reappears, it's crucial to ask yourself, "Why now? What does he want?"

- **The lesson here?** When dating today, it's essential that you pay attention! If a guy from your past reappears seemingly out of the blue, be cautious. Is he genuinely interested in reconnecting, or is he just looking for a quick fling? Don't be afraid to ask direct questions about what he's seeking in this renewed connection.

Lesson 2: Trust is earned, not given

Sometimes, there's a high cost when it comes to trust. Samson confided in Delilah, and she betrayed him. She used the knowledge of his weakness to deceive him, leading to his downfall. In dating today, this serves as a reminder of the cost of trusting too much too soon. Delilah was persistently trying to earn Samson's trust to discover his secret. Just as Mr. "Familiar" will persistently try to earn your trust quickly, he will then pursue you for sex. Samson thought he could trust Delilah, just like you might believe in the good intentions of someone you used to know. But Delilah was all about manipulation from the start, willing to do whatever it took to earn Samson's trust and get what she wanted.

- **The lesson here?** Don't readily give someone your trust just because they've been in your life before. Or even if someone from your past claims to have changed or swears they're different now, it doesn't mean you should immediately trust them. Trust should be earned over time through consistent actions and behavior. Delilah's betrayal is a harsh reminder that sometimes those who've hurt us in the past might do so again. Keep your guard up until you're sure they deserve it.

Lesson 3: Prioritize self-respect

Now, let's talk about the most critical lesson: self-worth and the power of choice. Delilah's relentless pursuit of Samson may have ultimately caused his downfall, but she didn't define his worth. Samson's choices were his own. Samson's downfall was directly related to his willingness to compromise his self-respect for Delilah. While on your dating journey, remember that your self-worth should be non-negotiable! Delilah finessed Samson, making him think he was in control. She used manipulation to get Samson to reveal his secrets, just as Mr. "Familiar" will try to entice you to lower your guard in order to sleep with you.

- **The lesson here?** Ladies, you have the power to make your choices. Remember, Mr. Familiar's actions don't define your worth or decisions. Take control of your dating life. If someone from your past tries to manipulate you, remember you hold the power. You decide who deserves a place in your heart and your life. If someone from your past attempts to deceive you or gain your trust through attention, gifts, etc., put your foot down and protect yourself. Don't be afraid to cut ties with those who don't have your best interests at heart.

Lesson 4: Guard Your Vulnerabilities

Samson fell for Delilah because he went against his better judgment and was too vulnerable. He opened up and revealed his secret, ultimately leading to his downfall. He let his guard down after developing feelings for Delilah and becoming too transparent, a.k.a. pillow talking too much. He was like an open book, and she read him like one.

- **The lesson here?** Not everyone from your past is out to deceive you. But when you're out there dating, it's essential to be open, honest, and cautious about baring it all too soon. You don't need to immediately share every detail of your life or body.

In the end, it's important to learn from Samson and Delilah's story. Their experience doesn't have to define yours, and even though Delilah acted deceitfully, not everyone from your past is like her. Unlike Samson, you must develop the ability to distinguish between someone who genuinely cares about you and someone who has ulterior motives. There are plenty of wonderful people out there seeking meaningful relationships, so don't let someone with hidden intentions discourage you from finding the love you deserve. The key is to recognize when manipulation is at play. They may not directly ask for your secrets or rush into physical intimacy, but they may leave subtle hints for you to see if you pay attention. By being aware of the patterns from your past, you can navigate relationships more consciously and protect your heart from those who would take advantage of your vulnerabilities. The "Delilah dilemma" is still relevant today. Samson's downfall resulted from ignoring warning signs; we can all learn from it. Don't become another Samson, allowing your past to control your future. Also, remember that not every man from your past deserves a place in your present or future. Remind yourself that the "Delilah effect" is real, but you have the power to recognize it and guard your heart. Don't let familiarity lead to your downfall. Keep your eyes open, stay true to your values, and find someone who genuinely respects and cherishes you for the long haul, not just in fleeting moments.

Quick ReCap: Reviewing the Misters

Let's take a moment to review the seven Misters and the various aspects of their personality traits, habits, and behaviors that you should consider avoiding when dating. This recap will help solidify your understanding of the seven Misters we recently discussed.

1. ***Mr. Dream Seller:*** He uses his storytelling abilities to create the illusion of romance or love, making women feel cherished and special. These seductive fantasies deeply resonate with women's desires, leading them to engage in short-term flings or remain in failing long-term relationships. He promises an exciting future together, which blinds women to the inconsistencies in his empty words. As they gradually lower their defenses, reality eventually sets in, causing disappointment. However, feelings had developed by then, and emotional intimacy had already been established.

2. ***Mr. Secretive:*** He's the type who keeps the important parts of his life hidden, like secret habits, lifestyle, STDs, children, side pieces, social media, etc. He doesn't show his true self when he first meets a woman. Instead, he

tells lies that captivate their curiosity, lowering their guard while avoiding transparency and honesty in relationships. There's no limit to what he will do in order to keep his agenda hidden and gain the trust of a woman.

3. **Mr. Aimless:** He thrives and takes advantage of women's nurturing qualities. This man may portray himself as a lost soul needing guidance and support. As he appears in need of the love of a good woman, he becomes a project for whoever he dates as they attempt to fix and support him. He seeks women who have a strong sense of direction in life. By doing so, he creates a dynamic where the woman is responsible for helping him better in his life. She thinks her love and encouragement can provide direction, but she steadily lowers her boundaries, believing she can help him find stability and meaning. However, in reality, she is compromising her boundaries, hoping to help him find his way, even though he lacks ambition.

4. **Mr. Hobosexual**: This man presents himself as a caring and supportive partner who needs emotional support, but he really needs a place to live. He shows vulnerability and a desire to settle down, suggesting that he's seeking love and a committed relationship. By doing so, he gains the trust of sympathetic women with low self-esteem, making them feel needed and important. The truth is, he's using her for financial support and convenience, all while withholding a full commitment. He may intentionally create a situation where she feels responsible

for caring for him, ultimately leading her to lower her boundaries and invest more in the relationship. Over time, he subtly relies on her for more support and contributions, gradually wearing out his welcome right before transitioning to his next victim and repeating the process.

5. ***Mr. Wolf in Sheep's Clothing:*** Mr. Wolf is like a manipulative chameleon pretending to be someone he is not to gain a woman's attention. He actively listens to the woman's needs and desires and appears to fulfill them by making her feel loved and secure. He exploits her emotions to gain her trust and devotion to achieve his hidden agenda (sex without commitment). Usually, by the time a woman learns his true intentions, her guard is already down, and she's deeply attached, causing emotional turmoil in the relationship.

6. ***Mr. Potential:*** He is a man who attracts women with his grand dreams and ambitions, painting a picture of a bright future she can be a part of. He creates an image that makes the woman in his life feel like she's the key to his success. However, he consistently fails to take concrete steps towards his goals, making her want to support and uplift him, hoping he will eventually achieve his dreams. His words keep her hopeful, and she may lower her boundaries, thinking he's just waiting for the right moment to commit. As women try to "fix" their lives, they become more intimately involved, lowering their self-worth in the process.

7. ***Mr. Familiar:*** Cleverly reaches out to past lovers, old coworkers, or classmates he's interested in. He then uses shared experiences to create an immediate sense of comfort and trust. He reminisces with women about the past, which triggers nostalgia and creates a fake sense of closeness. He tricks women into thinking they have a deep connection, making them more likely to lower their boundaries and become more open to intimacy with someone they already feel connected to.

Hopefully, now you better understand how each of the seven "Misters" uses manipulative tricks to deceive women. These tricks or mind games often lead women to go beyond their limits and get involved intimately without a committed relationship. The seven "Misters" exploit emotions, dreams, and shared experiences, making it difficult for women to see their true intentions. In the future, if you meet someone who appears too good to be true, take a step back, be cautious, and watch to see if he's showing any signs of these manipulation tactics. Don't be afraid to call them out and protect personal boundaries.

Chapter 8:

♟♞♝♜♛♚♝♞♟

Conclusion: The Girlfriend Treatment

W hile writing this book, I asked several single women two questions regarding their past relationships and dating experiences: "Have you ever been played before?" and "What do you think contributed to you not seeing the signs of the game that was successfully ran on you?" And despite these women being very emotionally intelligent individuals, they struggled to pinpoint an exact cause. When they asked my opinion, I advised them that the questions I asked were rhetorical. I explained that I was well aware of the answers because I was guilty of using them myself on unsuspecting women several times when I was single. I call it the *girlfriend treatment*. Simply put, the girlfriend treatment is when a man does everything in his power (temporarily) to make a woman feel special, loved, and cared for, unlike love bombing, which is a form of intense mind games and emotional abuse disguised as over-the-top flattery, extravagant gift-giving, or grand gestures.

The girlfriend treatment is more low-key and made to make a woman feel comfortable like she's in a loving, romantic relationship. This includes spending quality time together, being considerate, cooking meals together, providing emotional support, and paying attention to the details of her needs and wants. The girlfriend treatment aims to create a close and connected feeling, even if the people involved are not officially dating or in a committed relationship. All of the Misters mentioned in this book use this approach on some level. For instance, we have *Gary, the Dream Seller Type A,* he used the girlfriend treatment approach for a month, making an unsuspecting woman he met in a bar believe they were in a committed relationship and misleading her to engage in a short-lived fling, only to vanish after achieving his goal. Then we have *Tim, the Dream Seller Type B,* who used the girlfriend treatment to prolong a failing long-term relationship. He acted affectionately and partially committed, making his partner believe things were improving when, in reality, he was just doing the bare minimum to avoid a breakup. We can't forget *Wayne, the Hobosexual* and how he used it to trick a woman into moving him into her place after knowing him for a short while. He pretends to be the perfect boyfriend, making his host feel comfortable and secure, only to disappear once he no longer needs her accommodations. Lastly, there's *Secretive Gary,* who took things to another level by secretly using the girlfriend treatment on three different women simultaneously, without them knowing about each other. He manipulated them, fulfilling his lustful desires without any commitment.

Men of all types, appearances, and backgrounds have effectively utilized the girlfriend treatment to introduce women to relationship activities upfront, aiming to make them drop their guard and loosen their boundaries. Men do this to trick women into taking on the role of girlfriend, and do things that a girlfriend would do, without actually being in an exclusive relationship. When a man makes a woman feel like they've been played or tricked, it's usually because he has successfully used the girlfriend treatment to get what he wants. Now, let's look at how and why women react to the girlfriend treatment.

Recognizing the Signs

This dating approach involves more than just sending simple good morning texts or having the late-night conversations that typically happen after meeting someone. Guys who use the girlfriend treatment go a step further by intentionally including couple-like activities early on, making a woman feel like she's in a relationship without him committing. I understand that this might sound unrealistic or confusing, but simple activities such as planning and going on overnight trips, shopping together, and attending social or professional events are what couples usually do. The purpose of the girlfriend treatment is to make a woman feel as comfortable as possible so she's less likely to question the status of the relationship. That's why it affects you differently and catches you off guard when you get ignored or ghosted after experiencing this type of treatment. You end up realizing a reality that you never expected due to assumptions instead of clear knowledge about your relationship status. Fortunately, we can examine the two phases of the girlfriend treatment to better understand how it works effectively.

Phase one: This is all about your feelings and usually starts when a man you recently met puts in a lot of effort early on to make you feel like a girlfriend. Men have discovered that most women naturally act on what they hear and how they feel. Also, men learned that saying the right words in the right atmosphere will cause the average woman's emotions to spike, leading her to lower her boundaries. The key in Phase One is to shift the woman's attention towards the positive emotions she feels with him rather than clearly analyzing his actions or toxic traits. It becomes simpler for her to develop an emotional attachment without a relationship by making her feel incredibly happy during their time together. This emotional investment early on occasionally overshadows any warning signs or harmful behavior, making it harder to recognize the truth about the person she's dating.

Phase two: The focus is on a woman's reaction to the treatment. It's important to keep in mind that each woman might respond differently. Still, the most common response is to unconsciously act like a girlfriend and fully embrace the "Ride or Die Role" without requiring a commitment from the man involved. Once a man realizes that the woman has developed feelings for him and a strong physical attraction, her defenses weaken. At this point, most men start to back off and put in less effort because the woman has fully taken on the role of a committed partner, even assuming responsibilities typically associated with a "Ride or Die" girlfriend (cooking, spending money, having sex, meeting his needs, etc.). However, the man never establishes exclusivity and instead takes advantage of the woman's willingness to offer support. Although this approach has been proven effective, I know some of you might be thinking, "I already knew this," or "I know a man will say anything to sleep with women." While that may be true, I encourage you to take a moment and reflect on all the times you were ghosted after having sex with a man without knowing the true status of your relationship. Consider how he treated you before you gave in, and despite knowing what you claimed to know, he still persuaded you. I can assure you that this approach is responsible for every unexpected one-night stand or hit-it-and-quit-it, on and off again, a situation that you and many other women have experienced. It's why emotionally intelligent, responsible women find themselves three months and two-weekend trips in with a guy. Still unsure and still waiting for answers to their questions like, "What are we?" or "What are we doing?" I don't mean to sound cold, but trust me when I say that this approach is responsible for disarming countless women because it's extremely confusing and effective. Let's break down how to spot the differences between dating a man using the girlfriend treatment versus dating a man who's looking for a serious commitment. But before we do...

Pause for a moment and ask yourself:

1. Have you ever felt confused about the status of a relationship after experiencing couple-like activities early on? What signs did you miss that indicated it was just the girlfriend treatment?

2. Have you ever encountered the girlfriend treatment in your dating experiences, and did it leave you feeling confused or taken advantage of?

3. Can you identify a specific instance where a man used the girlfriend treatment to make you feel emotionally attached without a commitment? What were the warning signs you missed?

4. How do you personally respond to the emotional investment phase of the girlfriend treatment? Do you find yourself acting like a girlfriend without a clear commitment?

5. How can you be more assertive and straightforward in asking for clarity about the status of your relationship rather than assuming based on emotions?

6. How can you protect yourself from being played by someone using the girlfriend treatment? What steps can you take to ensure you're not mistaking a temporary emotional connection for a committed relationship?

Serious Commitment vs. the Girlfriend Treatment

Although it may not appear like it due to the nature of today's shallow dating pool, some decent, qualified men are seeking a real connection. But at the same time, there are also men who are using the girlfriend treatment as well. When you meet someone new, there are certain factors you should be aware of. These traits of men looking to use you are much different from those of someone actively seeking a serious, committed relationship. Understanding the differences between these two types of men allows you to make better choices about your love life. Here are the key points to consider when involved with a man using the girlfriend treatment compared to someone genuinely seeking a serious commitment. Firstly, consistent communication is non-existent with the men using the girlfriend treatment and often involves excuses or confusion. Unlike a man who wants to be in a committed relationship and who prioritizes speaking openly and honestly about his intentions. Secondly, plans for the future are vague, with a man using the girlfriend treatment. Instead of discussing and envisioning a shared future, his focus remains on living in the moment. Lastly, the emotional investment may differ significantly. While the girlfriend treatment can still involve an emotional connection, it may lack the depth and vulnerability experienced in a committed relationship. Let's explore the important aspects of dating a man who uses the girlfriend treatment and compare them to being with a man who wants a serious commitment.

Dating a Man Using the Girlfriend Treatment

1. **Intentions:**

    - **Girlfriend Treatment:** This type of man does not have long-term commitment or a serious relationship on his mind. His focus is more on casual dating, hooking up, or simply enjoying your company without any official commitment.

    - **Serious Commitment:** This type of man is actively looking for a committed, long-term relationship and is invested in slowly building a strong foundation with you for a future together.

2.   **Communication:**

- **Girlfriend Treatment:** There will always be a lack of clear communication about relationship expectations. He will avoid discussions about commitment, leading to uncertainty and confusion.

- **Serious Commitment:** He has no problem having open communication about his intentions, desires, and what he's seeking in a relationship. He is a man of his word; there is a mutual understanding of expectations and a desire to build a meaningful connection.

3.   **Emotional Investment:**

- **Girlfriend Treatment:** His level of emotional investment will vary; usually, he will do enough for sex or for most women to potentially become more emotionally connected and committed than he is. This can lead to differences in emotional satisfaction and fulfillment.

- **Serious Commitment:** He consistently displays a strong effort to nurture emotional bonding, reinforcing his commitment and creating a deeper connection grounded in trust and understanding.

Example of Dating a Man Using the Girlfriend Treatment

So, we've got Courtney and Jake. Courtney has her heart set on being in a relationship, investing her time and energy into what she assumes is something special, while Jake is pretending to play the role of the boyfriend of Courtney's desires. However, unknown to her, Jake meets all of Courtney's needs early on, treating her like a girlfriend without intending to commit. Although she cares about him, she is unsure about their future because Jake hesitates to take things to the next level. Yet she ignores her uncomfortable feelings (intuition) and keeps having a great time with him. They go on nice dates, chat freely, and are even planning trips together. The problem starts when it's time to confirm their relationship status, and Jake keeps avoiding it. He purposefully tiptoed around being exclusive, leaving Courtney in a state of limbo, caught in a web of mixed signals, questioning her self-worth, and wondering why he's not willing to make it official. When a guy uses the girlfriend treatment, his goal is to enjoy the perks of a physical connection without the responsibility of emotional commitment. He knows what to say and how to make his partner feel loved while he carefully avoids getting more deeply attached. Such confusing signals can make any woman question their self-value, making them wonder why he's so reluctant to make things official. The risk of continuing to invest time in hopes that he might change could potentially be wasted because there's a chance he may never act right.

So, what's the bottom line here? If you discover a man is giving you the girlfriend treatment, it's time to have a real conversation. Lay it all out, be honest about your feelings, and don't settle for being someone's temporary placeholder. If he gives you a line saying, "I'm not ready to commit," believe him, move on, and keep your heart open for someone on the same page.

Now let's examine what it's like to date a man who's actively seeking a serious commitment and how he provides a different experience defined by specific qualities and behaviors.

Dating a Man Seeking a Serious Commitment

1. **Clarity and Consistency:**

   - **Girlfriend Treatment:** Will always lack clarity and consistency. The man's actions and words never match. He creates confusion and uncertainty regarding his intentions and the future of the relationship.

   - **Serious Commitment:** He creates an environment of clarity that ensures consistent commitment through his words and actions. He will ensure that you and he are on the same page about his intentions and work with you to build a solid foundation for the future.

2. **Emotional Connection:**

   - **Girlfriend Treatment:** Emotional bonding for him is only temporary and not his core focus. His primary connection, if any, usually revolves around physical intimacy and sex rather than a deep emotional connection.

   - **Serious Commitment:** Establishing an emotional bond and compatibility are essential for him when building a relationship with a woman he's interested in. He aims to invest time, energy, and finances to create an authentic connection to strengthen their commitment to each other.

3. **Relationship Progression:**

- **Girlfriend Treatment:** The relationship will lack clear direction or a tangible plan for growth and the future, leading to a lack of progress. He will always keep you wondering, guessing, and stuck in the same spot.

- **Serious Commitment:** He has long-term visions, goals, and a plan for the future, and he doesn't mind sharing it with you. This will allow the relationship to grow and progress.

Example of dating a man seeking a serious commitment:

Rachel started dating Daniel, who's mature, responsible, and seeking that forever kind of love, you know? He desires a strong, steady relationship that stands the test of time, no matter how rough it gets. Rachel had the same wish, ready to shape her ways to match his. They vibed well, reflecting each other's emotions, basically in total sync. They shared overlapping life goals, shifting from 'mine' or 'yours' to 'our' achievements. Their shared path became visible through his commitment. This became a key development when the dreams about a combined journey started becoming a reality with their decision to commit to one another fully. What was vague previously became apparent due to shared work and mutual respect. The driving force behind their union was their truthful and caring attitude towards each other. Everyone knows that without trust, the ship will eventually sink, right? They agreed on how vital trust is in love. If it's missing, your love story could be torn down. Thus, they chose to stay real and honest with each other from day one. They relied on each other to build the basics of their relationship. With trust and honesty, along with mutual goals and commitment, they unlocked a blossoming love saga.

The story of Rachel and Daniel serves as a guide if you're after a devoted relationship. The following signs are the keys: (honesty, equal give and take, common goals, and accountability.) Measure your readiness for this relationship and align yourself with these factors. That's the best formula for a lasting, satisfying relationship. You can make more informed choices by understanding the contrasts between dating a man using the girlfriend treatment versus someone genuinely seeking a serious commitment. This understanding should enable you to align your dating preferences with someone who shares your commitment viewpoint in order for them to embark on nurturing and fulfilling partnerships that satisfy your demands. Here are some actionable steps to consider when you meet a man who consistently shows he wants a committed relationship:

Start a relationship with someone who wants commitment: This type of man will back up his words and embrace emotional growth and accountability. Find a partner who is enthusiastic about achieving a life-long connection.

Strive for emotional balance with your partner by listening to their feelings: Success in relationships depends greatly on compassion and understanding towards each other.

Plan your future considering common goals, not just personal ones: By focusing on "we" instead of "me" in making decisions, you create unity and celebrate successes together.

Focus on getting fully involved in the right relationship: Make compromises when needed to move together. When both people put effort into the relationship, it forms a deep connection and guides you down the same path.

Encourage Coevolution: The key to becoming a united force and developing a strong, long-term relationship is understanding, accountability, and respect. Your actions should reinforce the concept of "us," ensuring both of your goals stay aligned.

Look out for personal and shared interests equally: Balancing these aspects portrays respect and marks the trust and understanding that largely influence relationship dynamics.

Keep an open mind: Stay true to yourself while accepting your partner's flaws and strengths. Be real, keep conversation lines open, and don't be afraid to have "uncomfortable conversations" and be vulnerable. Honesty in words and actions builds up trust, which is crucial to having a relationship that lasts.

Peep Game: The Fork in the Road

Dating and relationships are important moments in life where your choices will significantly affect your love life. Whenever you meet a man on your dating journey, think of it as a fork-in-the-road moment! It's crucial in the beginning to recognize these key moments and make decisions based on your values. Each choice you make leads to a different path. You have choices like deciding whether to keep dating someone, setting relationship boundaries, committing more deeply, or reviewing your desires and needs. Dating is like a journey with many twists and turns leading to these fork-in-the-road moments. Making thoughtful decisions that align with your values, beliefs, and long-term goals is important. By acknowledging the impact of your decisions, you gain the power to approach dating more intentionally. When faced with choices, think about what's best for your peace of mind and future aspirations. Do your choices match your spiritual beliefs and vision of a satisfying life? Instead of seeing choices as burdensome, embrace them as opportunities to take control of your personal growth and self-discovery. Understand that every choice you make shapes your love life and has the potential to create a relationship that aligns with your lifestyle or sets you back. Remember, by embracing these moments, you can cultivate the potential for an intentional and fulfilling partnership. Always remember the inherent power of your choices, as they allow you to build relationships that truly nourish your soul.

Trusting and Listening to Your Inner GPS

In dating today, getting lost in the sea of swipes, messages, and countless first dates is easy. Finding the right path toward a meaningful and fulfilling connection can be challenging. Whether you know it or not, you possess an invaluable guide within yourself. I call it your inner GPS, aka your intuition. We would all agree that using a GPS to travel is essential for confirming we are headed toward a desired destination. Dating is no different. It's important to note that knowing where you want to go and who you want in the driver's seat is your responsibility. Just as you wouldn't hop in your car and blindly take a road trip with a stranger, the same applies to dating someone new. You must trust and utilize your inner GPS to help you find the type of relationship that's true to who you really are.

Sometimes, it can be tempting to let go of your values and ignore that inner voice telling you to "make a U-turn or you're going the wrong way!" Especially when you're head over heels or feeling the pressure to give in. You must realize that being mindful of your choices and listening to your inner GPS will help you stay true to yourself on your love journey. Have you ever gone on a date with someone who, on paper, seemed perfect, yet something in your gut told you otherwise? Listen and take heed to that feeling. Your gut instincts are powerful and your first line of defense against individuals with ulterior motives. If something feels off or uncomfortable, it's essential to acknowledge and investigate that feeling rather than dismissing it. Your gut feelings can help you avoid situations where someone might be using you for their gratification. Think of your intuition or inner voice as a superpower in dating. It's that feeling you get when something just doesn't sit right or when a connection with someone feels incredibly wrong. Your inner GPS is constantly helping you decide which paths are worth exploring and which ones you should steer clear of.

As a man, I can assure you that we, too, rely on our intuition when pursuing relationships. When you feel something is off or a situation doesn't align with your values, ladies, please listen to that instinct. Your inner voice is a trusted friend, always guiding you toward what's right for you. If you pay attention to it and make decisions consistent with your desires and aspirations, you'll be well-equipped to avoid falling for the deception of men who have less than honorable intentions. Relationships aren't pre-destined—they're choices you actively make. Every person you meet and get close to is a potential path on your love journey. Make decisions that are based on your virtues and what matters to you. Let your integrity guide you when you have to make a choice. For example, if you have two potential partners and one share your values while the other doesn't, go for the one who aligns with what's important to you. By doing that, you're build-ing a relationship that resonates with your beliefs. Dating today is full of twists and turns and the occasional dead end.

When you stop ignoring the signs, trust, and, more im-portantly, listen to your inner GPS, you can successfully navigate the roads of your love life. Your inner GPS is invaluable, helping you navigate the complexities of dating a man trying to run a game on you. It's there to protect you, guide you, and ensure you make choices that align with your well-being and values. Now that you understand how to identify men using the girlfriend treatment, you can now focus on men who value you for more than just your body and who are willing to give as much as you are. You're likely on the right path when you encounter a real one who respects your boundaries and values your thoughts and feelings. Trust the positive signals your inner GPS sends you and allow them to guide you toward healthy and fulfilling relationships. Likewise, when you notice a toxic trait or negative sign, trust your instincts and take them as warnings. Your inner GPS is continually working to help you make informed choices in the dating world.

Chapter 9:

Discernment 101

So, what is discernment and why is it essential in the world of dating? First, discernment is not just a fancy word for checking something out; it's defined as the ability to judge well. Unlike your intuition, which is your inner voice nudging you, discernment demands you take control, examine a situation carefully, and then make a final judgment. Discernment means you take your time to fully analyze and make sense of things that aren't clear. It's a skill that, over time, will strengthen your capacity to comprehend and make decisions about situations or grant a person access to your life. Especially if a person's intentions are hidden, misleading, or confusing; in other words, discerning someone you meet when dating protects you from being gullible and wasting your time. It's not about becoming a skeptic or shutting yourself off from the possibility of love. It's not about being judgmental; instead, it focuses on making clear choices that align with your vision of a fulfilling relationship. It's a delicate balance between openness and caution. Keep your eyes wide open, but also let your heart explore the possibilities presented to you. The art of discernment lies in finding that sweet spot.

Discernment vs. Being Judgmental

It's important to understand that using discernment and being judgmental, a.k.a. using hypocritical judgment, are like night and day, especially when it comes to dating. Discernment involves sound judgment, evaluating a situation objectively, considering risks, and making informed decisions with clarity. Hypocritical judgment is judging others while failing to hold yourself to the same standards. It frequently suffers from biases and unfair expectations. I discovered a perfect example of discernment in 1 John 4:1, which says, "Beloved, do not believe every spirit, but test these spirits, whether they are of God; because many false prophets have gone out into the world." Although the goal of that message was to prevent the church at the time from following false leaders, the same idea holds true when meeting new people (see chapter one of Peep Game: Testing for Pure Gold, where I explain how to use the acid test to assess a person's character). This statement urges us to never unquestionably trust every spirit or person we meet but instead analyze or test them to discern if they align with God or have your best interests at heart.

Before you grab your gavel and start judging harshly or without evaluating yourself first, I must bring to your attention another statement that Jesus made about being judgmental. Matthew 7:1-2 says, "Do not judge, or you too will be judged. For in the same way you judge others, you will be judged, and with the measure you use, it will be measured to you." Now, this is not an attack on judgment but a caution about the dangers of the hypocritical judgment of others and its consequences. He urges us to be mindful of our judgments, emphasizing self-awareness and fairness. While discernment is acknowledged, the verse emphasizes humility and self-reflection in assessing others. Using discernment while dating encourages individuals to make informed judgments about a relationship's potential, considering emotional, physical, and spiritual compatibility. It involves observing and understanding someone's character, intentions, and actions without jumping to hasty conclusions. It's about being perceptive, asking thoughtful questions, and truly listening to the person you're getting to know. When you exercise discernment, you assess and evaluate whether your values align with each other before getting more serious. On the flip side, using hypocritical judgment while dating stems from preconceived notions, societal pressures, or personal insecurities. This can lead to making judgments quickly and disapprovingly. Forming harsh opinions and criticisms, often without being open-minded. In other words, you don't want to impose rigid standards on a potential partner without considering your flaws or shortcomings. This can lead to unfair comparisons, unrealistic expectations, and a tendency to dismiss someone based on superficial reasons.

The Foundation: Know and Become the Best Version of Yourself

You've probably heard it before, but it's worth repeating: Know yourself! One powerful aspect of developing your 'deal breakers' and 'must-haves' lists is the need to embody the qualities and values you seek in a partner. It's a two-way street. If you expect respect, you must also offer respect. If you seek open communication, you must also be willing to engage in it. This principle extends beyond mere compatibility; it's about personal growth and authenticity. When you become the person you want to attract, you enhance your discernment and attract individuals who genuinely match your values. Understanding yourself, your values, your dreams, and what makes you tick is important before inviting someone else into your life. Take time to reflect on your past relationships, identifying good and bad patterns. This self-awareness will serve as your guide on your dating journey. You must embark on an inner quest for self-awareness and make every effort to become the best version of yourself to attract a partner who reflects your lifestyle and ideals. In other words, you must understand what you truly want and require in a relationship. Reflect: Ask yourself tough questions to identify your core values, passions, and aspirations, and also consider your non-negotiable aspects. Remember, focusing on self-improvement will naturally attract individuals who resonate with your authentic self. Before discerning others, it's important first to understand yourself. To build a strong foundation for discernment, you should not only create a "deal breakers" and "must-haves" list for potential partners but also create one for yourself and work on making the improvements. Let's look at some examples that can assist you with your personal development.

Deal Breakers for Yourself: Identify the traits or behaviors within yourself that you find unacceptable. It could be a tendency to avoid difficult conversations or a habit of trusting too soon. By addressing these deal breakers, you enhance your life and set a positive example for your future partner.

Must-Haves for Yourself: Similarly, list the qualities you want to cultivate within yourself. If you value kindness, make a conscious effort to practice kindness in your daily life. If you desire open communication, work on expressing yourself honestly and transparently.

Think about your core principles, passions, and life goals. Think about how you want to improve your personal growth and continuously work on nurturing the qualities that matter to you. Attracting the right person starts with being the right person. Just as you have deal breakers and must-haves for potential partners, consider creating some for yourself.

The Ripple Effect

The beauty of embodying the qualities you seek in a partner can only add to the quality of your romantic relationship. It influences all aspects of your interactions with the men you meet. Your authenticity becomes a magnet for building deeper and more meaningful connections. The process of becoming the person you want to attract is not about changing yourself to fit someone else's mold; it's about embracing the best version of yourself. It's a journey of self-improvement, self-awareness, and self-love. This isn't a one-time task but an ongoing process. Your desires and values might shift as you evolve, upgrade, and grow. Embrace this evolution, adapt, and continue to embody the qualities that resonate with your desired relationships. Ultimately, authenticity and alignment with your core values will create a powerful ripple effect, attracting individuals who match your aspirations and support your personal growth. It's about nurturing relationships built on a strong foundation of shared values and authenticity, leading to deeper, more fulfilling connections.

Using Discernment While Dating: Tools for Making Empowered Choices

Now that you understand the difference between discernment and hypocritical judgment, how exactly do you discern a potential partner? First, no one else can complete you; your wholeness comes from within. Embrace the power of discernment as you navigate your dating journey. In this chapter, we embarked on a journey of self-discovery and developing discernment. By using these two tools together, Deal Breakers and Must Haves, as well as Comparing Values and Behaviors, you'll unlock the key to avoiding wasteful encounters, finding true compatibility, and protecting your heart. This is based on wisdom from Matthew 7:17–20, which says the following: "Likewise, every good tree bears good fruit, but a bad tree bears bad fruit. A good tree cannot bear bad fruit, and a bad tree cannot bear good fruit. Every tree that does not bear good fruit is cut down and thrown into the fire. So then, by their fruit you will recognize them."

Tool One: Deal Breakers and Must-Haves

Imagine building your dream relationship like a grand bridge, one brick at a time. The foundation of this structure lies in creating a detailed blueprint: your unique combination of deal breakers and must-haves lists. Before you start getting to know someone new, I encourage you to have a clear understanding of what you're looking for in a partner. This isn't about creating an unrealistic checklist but identifying your non-negotiables and the qualities that align with your values. Take a moment to think about yourself. Consider what matters most to you in a relationship. What are the things you value and can't give up on? What qualities do you need for a strong and meaningful connection to grow truly? These questions are really important for making wise choices and having a satisfying relationship. Creating well-defined deal breakers and must-haves lists empowers you to set boundaries and preserve your dignity. These lists will significantly contribute to the discernment process on your dating journey.

Your Deal Breakers list contains the non-negotiables, the boundaries you set to protect your heart. Take time to jot down the things you absolutely cannot compromise on. Maybe it's values, habits, or certain behaviors. It could be incompatible with life goals to display physical or verbal abusive tendencies. Whatever they are, be firm in your convictions. Your deal breakers will act as a filter, helping you sift through potential time wasters. These are the warning signs that, if present, should send you running in the opposite direction. In other words, if you prefer an easy-going type of guy and discover your potential partner is argumentative, shows signs of having a temper or, is easily angered, and becomes overly possessive, that's a deal-breaker. If you dream of building a family, but he's allergic to the idea of commitment or having kids, that's a deal-breaker. Do you value respect and integrity the most? Write down these deal breakers, making sure they're clear and prioritized. Remember, discernment allows you to say no to relationships that compromise your happiness and integrity.

Even beyond protection, your must-haves list includes the qualities and attributes a potential partner must possess to create a fulfilling connection. Your must-haves list isn't about creating the perfect image of a partner. Consider what values are essential to you. Is kindness a must-have? Shared interests or hobbies? Emotional intelligence? Write down the qualities you absolutely must have in a potential partner. Again, be specific. If humor is essential to you, list it. If having a stable career or intellectual compatibility matters, ensure they're on the list. Document these traits clearly, assigning them appropriate importance. By doing so, you'll establish a framework that helps you navigate potential relationships, starting from a place of confidence. Armed with the power of your deal breakers and must-haves lists, combined, you can pave a path that sidesteps a potential Mister and forge deep connections. Take pride in knowing that your discernment, rooted in self-awareness, will guide you on the unpredictable road of modern dating. Remember to be patient, as discernment requires careful observation and self-reflection. As you make empowered choices, feeling deserving of the love and connection you seek, be confident that you will find your person.

Bringing It All Together

Imagine you're on a date with someone new and have your deal-breakers and must-haves tucked away in your mind. You're observing their actions, comparing them to their words, and assessing whether their values align with yours. You're also mindful of your growth, actively working on being the person you want to attract.

Example: Let's say your date makes a comment that raises a potential concern that touches on one of your deal breakers. Instead of brushing it aside, you take a moment to reflect. Is this a one-time occurrence, or is it part of a larger pattern of behavior? You trust your instincts and decide to address them openly and honestly by saying, "Hey, I couldn't help but notice when you mentioned [a specific topic]; it raised some concerns for me. Can we talk about it?" This open and direct communication allows your date to explain themselves and sets the tone for healthy communication in the relationship. It's a proactive approach to discernment.

Tool Two: Comparing Values and Behaviors

Now, let's discuss the second tool in your discernment toolkit—comparing values and behaviors. This involves a bit of observation and introspection, and it's inspired by a timeless piece of advice found in the aforementioned Matthew 7:17–20. In the context of dating, this passage encourages us to pay attention to the actions, or fruit, of the person we're considering as a potential partner. Are they consistent in displaying positive behaviors, or do negative behaviors continuously pop up? It's about looking beyond the words and assessing the substance of their true character. When applying this ancient wisdom to dating, you must focus on observing a potential partner's values and their life's philosophy and assessing whether they align with their actions. Pay close attention to how they treat others, their consistency in displaying compassion, honesty, and respect, and how they live. Actions reveal a person's character more truthfully than mere words or intentions ever could. It's easy for someone to talk, but do their actions match their words? Are they consistent, or do you notice patterns of behavior that raise concerns?

Bringing It All Together: Fruit Inspection

The analogy of trees and their fruit is a powerful metaphor for understanding the essence of a person. Just as a healthy tree yields good fruit, a person with good character and intentions will exhibit positive qualities in their actions and behavior. As a result, someone with negative traits will display "bad fruit," signifying undesirable behaviors or intentions. Let's break down this biblical advice and see how it can be a guiding light in your dating journey:

Recognize them by their fruits:

When you're trying to form opinions about someone new, be careful. Just as in the biblical context, be cautious of those who present themselves as something they're not. The things they say might not always represent who they truly are. That's why paying attention and looking for real evidence of their positive or negative qualities is important. The key is to pay close attention to how someone treats you and others, especially in difficult or stressful situations. How do they handle conflicts? Do they show kindness and empathy? Are they respectful, even when no one is watching? These behaviors are the fruits you should be examining. In the dating world, this could mean someone who projects an image of kindness and sincerity but fails to demonstrate these qualities in their actions. By carefully observing their actions, you will learn valuable information about their true character and make better judgments.

Healthy trees = good fruit.

Imagine a strong and healthy tree that is well taken care of and has plenty of resources to grow. Similarly, when a person follows good principles and values, they tend to show positive character traits. These values and principles are like the roots of a tree; they shape its identity and influence what it does. When you meet someone who has the same beliefs, it means you both can benefit from a shared understanding of what is important. This shared value system plays a big role in how a person behaves and makes decisions that directly affect you. Let's take honesty as an example. If honesty is important to you, chances are you will recognize it in others who value it, too. These people will consistently show integrity and reliability through honest words and actions, with little effort, if any. Just like a strong tree produces delicious fruits organically, a person who holds positive values and principles will naturally show admirable behavior. That's why seeking out like-minded individuals is important on your dating journey.

Bad Trees = Bad Fruit.

On the flip side, if there's a misalignment in values, beliefs, and principles, it is important to pay close attention to the actions that might cause worry. Matthew 7:19 warns, "Every tree that does not bear good fruit is cut down and thrown into the fire." In the context of dating, this verse suggests that individuals who consistently display negative behavior or character should be recognized for who they are and not given the opportunity to cause harm or disappointment. Recognizing the "bad fruit" early in the dating process allows you time to cut them off to save yourself from potential heartache and protect yourself from harmful relationships. It is wise to rely on your instincts, as they often serve as trustworthy signals. If something doesn't feel right, it's probably because it isn't. Trust yourself and be vigilant for the signs. When it comes to dating, it's important to evaluate someone's character based on how they behave and what they value. Matthew 7:15–20 provides a profound lesson that can assist you in your dating journey. By paying attention to a man's character and actions, you can effectively discern whether he is a "bad tree" bearing "bad fruit" or a "good tree" bearing "good fruit." The metaphor underscores the importance of aligning a person's character with their behavior and being cautious of those who wear a fake facade. You can learn much about a person by observing how they treat others and handle everyday situations. Finding someone who shares your values and principles is important for building a healthy relationship. It is vital to remember that dating is a discovery process, and not every person will be a perfect match. However, by applying the wisdom of this biblical passage, you can become more knowledgeable about recognizing genuine, kind-hearted men while avoiding those who may pose a threat to your emotional well-being. In the pursuit of meaningful and healthy relationships, discernment is a valuable tool that should be used at all costs without fear or compromise.

Peep Game: Rewrite The Rules

We talked about how tricky it can be to navigate modern dating and how to steer clear of manipulative tactics often used by the different Misters. To rewrite the dating rules, you must first equip yourself with self-awareness using intelligence and emotional insight. This will help you embody the traits you're looking for in a partner. Emotional intelligence is the key to reading between the lines and gauging whether a potential partner is truly ready for commitment. Emotional intelligence is knowing your feelings, understanding the reasons behind them, sharing them openly, and managing your emotions in a way that adds value to the relationship. Only you can decide what you want and deserve in order to confidently eliminate those who don't appreciate you or your search for a sincere, enduring connection. You can take charge and rewrite the rules—no more accepting flimsy excuses, waiting endlessly for a text response, or dealing with confusing mixed signals. Speak your mind, stay true to yourself, and focus on connecting with someone who fits your life goals early on to avoid mismatched expectations. Having a clear approach, free from assumptions, helps you avoid staying in a failing relationship due to fear and insecurity. This is not just about finding a spouse; it's about laying the groundwork for a future graced with mutual respect, deep connection, and, yes, lasting romance. The new rules of dating are not crafted from deceit or luck. But understanding the importance of not settling for less, holding high standards, keeping a moral compass, and dating with a clear purpose enables you to be part of relationships where those values are mutually respected.

Dating with Purpose for the Marriage-Minded Woman

Let me share some advice on how to keep an eye on finding a man who reflects your desire to date with purpose while avoiding giving too much too early or doing "wifely duties" just because you're in love. First, dating with purpose doesn't mean you're desperate to tie the knot or trying to fix how lonely and down on yourself you might feel. Dating with this mindset means you're willing to be upfront about looking for a serious, long-term relationship that will lead to marriage. It's not that every date has to be super serious, especially not the first few. But it would be best to let your dates know what you're looking for. A good match will appreciate this honesty and be on the same page, but if he doesn't, it lets you move on without wasting your time. Here's the thing: when you know what you want, you filter out any potential "Misters" who are just looking for a casual fling. Dating with purpose is a term people throw around without giving it much thought. This mindset isn't about prematurely taking on the role of an unofficial wife or wifey by doing things only married couples should do because it will reduce your worth as time passes (trust me). If you catch yourself acting like you're already married just because you're in your feelings, think twice. Relationship responsibilities should happen because you both really care about each other and are committed—not because you feel like you have to prove your love. Don't exchange love and affection for attention or special treatment in a relationship that isn't serious yet. You deserve someone who truly values you. Really, dating with purpose means you're ready for a real commitment and expect the same back. To wrap up, want-ing a serious relationship or marriage should come from careful thought, not rushing or stress. It's about being real, holding on to what you value, and meeting someone special who naturally wants to be with you for life. Look for a relationship where both people respect each other, share their dreams, and take their future seriously. Make sure you both give back as much love and effort as you put in.

No Settling Allowed

Listen up! The days of lowering your expectations or selling yourself short are done and dead. One of the essential rules to rewrite is this one: never settle for less! I'm sure you've heard that saying countless times without giving it any thought. Settling happens when you compromise on your core values or what you truly want in a partner, thinking you won't find someone better. Even though the world might throw a bunch of options at you, some shine brighter than others. Never mistake shining for sub-stance. In other words, it's not about being unrealistic; it's about knowing your worth and holding out for someone who sees it too. Imagine for a moment that you're at a restaurant. You order your favorite dish, but they bring you something completely dif-ferent. Are you just going to accept it and eat it quietly? No way! You'd send it back and expect what you asked for. The same goes for relationships. If someone's not giving you what you deserve, it's okay to say, "This isn't what I ordered," and send it back. Let's go deeper and talk about the importance of not settling for less. First, you must understand what you bring to the table, and don't ever allow yourself to become someone's backup plan. If a guy's not meeting your needs, doesn't align with your values, or mistreats you, it's time to show him the door. That's non-negotiable. Why are you entertaining the idea if he doesn't make you feel like the main attraction? Never attempt to change yourself or sacrifice your dignity just to make things work with the wrong person. Cutting off someone not meeting your needs isn't being mean or demanding—it's self-respect. Don't be afraid to upgrade and walk away from situations that don't honor your worth. Your time is too precious for anything less than to receive genuine respect and care.

Nowadays, there's this misconception that being in a relationship—any relationship—is better than being alone. But that's not true. You don't want to talk yourself into accepting less and having a man around just as a filler. He might be handsome and tatted up with a six-pack, but if he doesn't add value to your life by making you smile, encouraging your dreams, or sharing a connection, he's just taking up space. Sometimes, though, I get it; your inner voice might whisper, "He's kind of good enough," or "I may not find anyone better." This mindset is wrong because it encourages fear, makes you comfortable, and glorifies mediocrity in your love life when you want to vibe with excellence. The moment you're okay with just 'alright' or 'good enough' is when you've sold yourself short because settling will only lead to disappointment in the long run. Being in a below-average relationship with a below-average man shouldn't be the goal. It's just ridiculous to think you shouldn't expect the best. I'm sure you want more than just okay, right? Now, let's flip the script. Think of dating as casting a superhero for your blockbuster. You're in the director's chair, and let's face it, the casting is full of actors with potential, but not everyone's cut out to be the leading role. You're screening for a co-star who resonates with the theme of your life, who hits those marks, knows his lines, and can keep up with your pace. And for that role, you need an A-lister—someone with depth and integrity who loves you without demanding a rewrite of your character.

From now on, treat each encounter as a lesson and every relationship as a chapter. Grow from them, but never lose yourself in them, and certainly don't downplay your unique qualities to be with someone below average. The right one will admire you for being who you are. Remember, this dating thing is not about wearing down or giving in. It's about holding out and pressing on, understanding that what you allow is what will continue. So, what's it gonna be? Well, that's for you to decide. But between me and you, there's only forward from here. A forward where you never settle for less but always for what stirs your soul and makes you feel unapologetically and generously loved. Rewrite the rules, peep-game, and find someone who's not just playing but is coming to win this with you, side by side.

Pause for a moment and ask yourself:

1. How do you find the sweet spot where your standards are high enough to demand respect but flexible enough to let a good man show you his true potential?
2. How do you communicate your non-negotiables when dating without coming off as defensive or unapproachable?

3. How do you define your worth in the dating market without selling yourself short or setting unreachable expectations?

4. How do you maintain composure and prevent their strong chemistry from obscuring your standards when you first meet someone and feel that instant connection?

5. What does 'setting high standards' in dating mean to you personally, and how does that reflect in your choices of whom to date?

Keep Those Standards and Morals High

Let's cut to the chase. This topic can be downright challenging because our generation shies away from the idea that morals and standards are important. Even more shockingly, women are dating today expecting a positive outcome without considering the role standards and morals play in the process. Having standards and morals isn't about being picky; it's about knowing which behaviors fit with your sense of right or wrong and your core beliefs about how you should be treated and how you should treat others. Ignoring these principles while dating can often lead to regret. To compromise is one thing, but when you constantly cross your moral boundaries, you might find yourself on paths that don't lead you where you truly want to go. Paths where you ultimately get used for your body and then ghosted. Paths of verbal and physical abuse or wasting years of your life in a dead-end relationship. That's why having standards will protect your integrity and help create a mindset where you treat your body like a treasure. This isn't about gatekeeping your intimacy but rather understanding your self-worth. When you value yourself, you're less likely to give away pieces of that treasure on a whim. It's about ensuring someone truly values and resonates with the entirety of who you are—including the moral standards you uphold—before you invite them into a more intimate space (physically and emotionally). And trust me, when a man recognizes a woman who knows her worth—crafted carefully through those morals and standards—it's a game-changer. Respect attracts respect.

Raising these barriers may reduce your dates, but deciding to refine potential partners promises more quality than quantity. Think of what's right and wrong for you—these ideas often come from your thoughts, culture, or mindset. They might be tough to see, but they are a big part of what makes you who you are, and they'll help you choose when you've got decisions to make. Keeping true to these beliefs affects who you allow to come into your life. For example, consider honesty—a moral that often ranks at the top of many people's lists. When you prioritize transparency and seek it actively in your connections, you attract individuals who value the truth as much as you do. Suppose you neglect an honest interaction for the appeal of physical attraction. In that case, several things can happen—misunderstandings due to a lack of communication, a foundation built on half-truths, and, ultimately, deeper heartbreak when the truth emerges. Creating and upholding standards while dating means deciding what you find okay and what you want for yourself in a relationship. If your standard is to date someone who's committed and puts in the effort, you'll likely avoid investing time in someone who shrugs off plans or doesn't show any real interest.

Let's say your friend meets a guy who initially seems qualified. However, she has a set of particular standards, especially when she meets someone attractive. She knows that fun dates are cool, but he should focus on getting to know each other better. So, as soon as this guy is hit with her standards and starts being iffy with his texts, avoids talking about where the relationship is heading, or expects her to change plans while he keeps doing whatever he wants, these are warning signs. She notices them and cuts him off immediately because of the standards she's made and won't overlook. Standards like these acts as filters that separate a potential life partner from a potential life lesson. Think of it like currency in the dating market—raising your value in such a way that you're only spending it on worthwhile investments. Peep game, make Queen moves, and hold fast to the morals that guide you and the standards that support the integrity of who you are. They are more than mere safeguards against heartbreak and the Mr. Wrongs in the dating wilderness; they're guiding lights that attract the likes of Mr. Right and those who hold high regard for them, harnessing harmony, respect, and maybe your very own happily ever after.

The End

Milton Keynes UK
Ingram Content Group UK Ltd.
UKHW020449220424
441235UK00006BB/37

9 798892 986625